Other books by the authors:

Far-Out Ideas for Youth Groups
Right-On Ideas for Youth Groups
Way-Out Ideas for Youth Groups
Fun-N-Games
Super Ideas for Youth Groups
Holiday Ideas for Youth Groups
Incredible Ideas for Youth Groups

Compiled by
Wayne Rice
Denny Rydberg
and
Mike Yaconelli

Zondervan Publishing House
Grand Rapids, Michigan

FUN-N-GAMES
Copyright © 1977 by Youth Specialties

Zondervan Publishing House, 1415 Lake Drive, S.E., Grand Rapids, Michigan 49506

Library of Congress Cataloging in Publication Data

Rice, Wayne.
  Fun-n-games.

  1. Games.   2. Recreation.   3. Group games.
I. Yaconelli, Mike, joint author.   II.   Rydberg, Denny, joint author.   III.   Title.
GV1201.R44   790   77-21854
ISBN 0-310-35001-8

The authors wish to express their appreciation to the many churches, youth groups, and youth organizations whose creativity made this book possible.

Printed in the United States of America

84   85   86   87   88 — 20   19   18   17   16   15   14   13   12

CONTENTS

FOREWORD

This is a game book. But it is more than that. It is a *Fun*-N-Game book. *Fun-N-Games* is not the typical, boring, jock-oriented game book featuring 400 games no one likes to play. The games in this book are fun. And anyone may play them regardless of age, sex, ability, or dexterity (you don't even have to know what dexterity means). We even left out all technical jargon, measurements, and complicated rules that normally accompany a game book. You might even find the book itself fun to read.

All we've tried to do is describe as many games as we could as simply as possible so you can have a good time. After all, that's what games are all about — having a good time. We hope you have fun playing the games in this book. We hope you will catch a glimpse of something that has almost been lost in the highly competitive American culture — the joy of gameplaying.

Each game in *Fun-N-Games* was chosen on the basis of specific criteria. The criteria we used to *include* games in this book are probably the same criteria used by most game books to *exclude* games from theirs. That's because the criteria we used have nothing to do with winning or skill. Every game was chosen for its potential for contributing towards community. We think games are celebration, not warfare, and, therefore, ought to bring people together rather than separate them. The following is a list of the criteria we used:

7

Competition

Competition is not inherently evil. Every game in this book
does involve some competition, but the overriding emphasis is
not on winning. Winning is either irrelevant or anti-climactic.
Competition, as we see it, is only valid if it increases the
enjoyment of each participant. If competition results in driving
a wedge between the "good" and the "bad," or the "skilled"
and "non-skilled," then it is destructive and not useful. Competition may occur between teams, individuals, or an external
record or ideal. But when competition gets in the way of play,
then the game is too competitive. In this book, even in the
games where there are "winners," the honor is dubious. After
all, how distinctive is it to be declared the winner of the
"Knee-Knock Relay"?

Unskill

We chose games that tend to equalize everyone so that all
participants have an equal chance to win. Either the games
require no skill or they require skills that no one has ever heard
of. That's why we excluded football and included the Armpit-
Egg Relay. There aren't too many people skilled at holding an
egg in their armpit. In fact, there aren't too many people who
want to be skilled at holding an egg in their armpit.

Adaptability

Games may be played anywhere. At least the ones in this book.
    Many people can't play a game unless they play by the
"official" rules, on an "official" playing field with "official"
equipment. That's too bad because those people miss the fun of
gameplaying. Although we would agree that many games are
played best under certain conditions, any game may be
adapted to fit *any* condition. If rain keeps you from having a
relay event outside then shift the games to inside and change
the rules to accommodate a gym floor where street shoes may
not be worn. (i.e., instead of running, pull the kids on blankets). If you want to play baseball and the field is too small, then
change the ball to a mushball or volleyball. Adaptability simply

means that games were made to be played, and, therefore, whatever has to be done to get people to play and enjoy them, can and should be done.

First String

There is no such thing as second string. Every game in this book may be played by anyone. The only qualification is a willingness to play.

Seasons

There are no seasons for any of the games in this book. In the first place, few people have heard of most of our games and we doubt there is a real danger of the "Waddle Walk" becoming a national pastime. When you play a game is determined by you, not the season.

Energy

Who wants to play if they can't play hard? That is a good question because many people (especially jocks) assume that if a game is fun it's for sissies because the game requires little or no effort. Nothing could be more incorrect.

We chose games that required maximum effort with minimum risk. And because the skills required in these games are not related to physical size and strength, there is a great deal of energy demanded from the participants in the form of new skills. This results in an atmosphere of healthy intensity, fun, and community.

Choice

We attempted to include games not only fun to play but fun to watch. There is a reason for that. We believe people ought to have the option to play or not to play. It is crucial to the success of gameplaying that the participants *want* to play. But it is also important that there be *no qualitative distinction between player and spectator.*

If a game is enjoyable to watch, then even those who observe are a part of the game.

Choice also implies that games should not have fixed limits for teams or players. Thus, if someone decides to play or drop out, the game may be stopped and the teams adapted to accommodate the new situation.

Choice also means that more than one game may be played at the same time. The more games offered at the same time, the better the chances everyone will find a game he is motivated to play. Of course, it is much easier to get full participation if the games are fun, non-threatening, and non-skilled.

Fun-N-Games represents a new direction in recreational philosophy — unskilled, competitive gaming. Without a doubt, this book will have tremendous influence on the recreational philosophy of the future. Every one of the ideas in *Fun-N-Games* has been used successfully by groups across the North American continent as well as many foreign nations.

CREATIVE GAME MAKING

A game is something that can be created by anyone. And that means *you!* There is no international game cartel with a monopoly on new games. Anyone is qualified to create his own games. All it takes is a practical application of a few simple brainstorming principles and you'll soon have a whole notebook full of original games.

Creative gamemaking involves either the *construction* of a completely new game from scratch or the *reconstruction* of an existing game. But the principles are the same for both.

Let's take a somewhat common situation to illustrate the brainstorming process. You are in charge of recreation for a high school summer camp. The grass field is not adequate for open field games and the volleyball court is constantly being used. The volleyball net is somewhat worn and almost at "official height" (whatever that is). But the only people enjoying volleyball are the jocks who have monopolized every game. The problem is obvious and much too common. How can you change the game so that *everyone* may actively participate (including the jocks) and still have fun?

1. Analyze the problem. If you describe the problem by prefacing it with "in what ways might I?", it becomes much easier to focus on the problem. For instance, "In what ways might I de-emphasize the presence of the jocks?" Or, "In what ways might I increase enthusiasm in the group?" Or, "In what ways might I get more people involved?" As you isolate simple

11

elements of the problem rather than the one big problem, the solutions become much more possible.

2. Take the analysis one step further. Ask *why* to each of the "In what ways might I" questions. For example, you already have the question, "In what ways might I de-emphasize the presence of the jocks?" Now ask, "*Why* do I want to de-emphasize the presence of the jocks?" Possible answers might include: because they jump too high, they hog the ball, they're too strong, they're all over the court, no one else can hit the ball, etc. Now you have some handles on the problem that enable you to tackle possible solutions with a passion.

3. Brainstorm wildly for solutions. For brainstorming to be successful you must keep in mind the four cardinal rules of brainstorming: (1) *Criticism is ruled out.* No idea should be rejected regardless of how "irrelevant it sounds." No one should comment on the quality of the ideas suggested. (2) *Free wheeling is welcome.* Be as bizarre as you want in the beginning. You can always drop or adapt bad ideas later. (3) The emphasis is on *quantity, not quality.* Just list all the ideas suggested in the order given and don't worry whether they make sense. The more ideas you generate the greater the number of good ideas *and* the greater number of lousy ideas you'll generate. The important thing is to get lots of ideas to work with. (4) Now that you have filled the blackboard or paper with ideas, *refine, combine, and improve* what you have until you arrive at a number of possible solutions.

Let's continue with the volleyball situation and the domineering jocks. As a result of the brainstorming process, we have decided that the jocks hog the ball, jump too high, run all over the court, etc. Hence, some possible solutions:

— raise the net to fifteen feet (no one can spike over that)

— change the ball into a weather balloon, water balloon, giant pushball, nerfball, balloons tied together, Ping-Pong ball, etc.

— lower the net to a foot off the ground

— change the number of people who have to hit the ball

before it goes over — everyone on the team, two boys and two girls, etc.

— tie people together; have them hold hands

— have them stand on one foot, sit, lie down, stand with backs to the net, on their knees, etc.

— blindfold the players

— use a solid cloth for the net so it is impossible to see on the other side

— water down the field, play in mud, water

— make the points the amount of times both teams hit the ball continuously without stopping

These are just a few ideas. But if you are like we are, you already ought to be excited about the possibilities. Volleyball will never be the same again, and why should it be when you have so many fun alternatives?

Of course, some problems are not so easy to solve and many groups don't think they can think of anything. Therefore, we would like to suggest some gimmicks you can use to stimulate imagination.

1. Look in your wallet. Sounds odd, but it isn't. Search through your wallets and use what's in them to stimulate imagination. Let's take the volleyball game again. You find a telephone credit card and as a result you begin to brainstorm — wires, phones, calling, messages, money, telephone numbers, bells, long distance. From a list of words like that you might come up with these suggestions: change the distance between the teams, or players; wire the legs of two players together; referee calls out number of players who have to hit the ball as ball crosses net, etc.

2. What's your hobby? Suppose someone suggests mac-rame. From that you could create a lot of ideas — for example, have each player catch the ball in some kind of net, have the entire team hold a blanket and use it to catch and return the ball over the net.

3. Miscellaneous. Think about favorite places or events like

the circus or Gran Prix; magnify or minimize any aspect of a game (Ping-Pong ball to weather balloon, or vice versa), and finally, think in terms of rearranging things.

Of course, we have only touched the surface, but you should still know enough about brainstorming now to create your own Fun-N-Games book. The important thing is to realize you have the potential to create your own games. We even think you'll find gamemaking as fun as gameplaying.

CREATIVE GAME PLANNING

There is much more to being a good recreation person than merely owning a book full of great new games (meaning this one). Without a considerable amount of thought, preparation, and sensitivity, you always stand a good chance of disappointment, frustration, or failure. We can't guarantee success, but we can sure give you some helpful suggestions to *almost* guarantee it.

How to Choose the Right Game

A book full of Fun-N-Games can complicate your life when it comes to selecting a game. We think every game in this book is worth playing. But because each group is different and each situation is different, certain games are better than others. We hope the check list below will help you choose the "right" game for you.

1. Age of group. Amost every game in this book may be played by *any* regardless of age, but there are certain games more suitable for specific ages. If you are planning games for families, then choose games involving cooperation and little physical contact. If you want some games for high school boys, then choose some good physical contact games requiring maximum energy.

2. Sex. Generally it's best to separate the sexes for physical, hard-hitting games. That doesn't mean girls can't play physical games, it just means it's best if they don't play co-ed. If you like

15

couples' games, make sure you have enough of each sex to allow for all the couples needed.

3. Size. Some games like "John-john" and "Pull Up" don't play very well in a small group; but others, like "Anatomy Shuffle," "Balloon Basketball," etc., do. Just make sure you recognize the difference.

4. Personality. Every group has a unique personality (group dynamics and all that stuff). Some are active, outgoing, and physical, while others are more easygoing and "sophisticated." Of course, it's good to give any group new experiences, but it's also good to start with something you know they will feel comfortable with. Choose games that your group can really enjoy, not just games that are fun for *you*.

5. Ability. Even though all the games in this book require no particular ability, or unheard-of skills, there are some things people cannot do. Little children have a difficult time balancing cups of water on their heads. Older people have a hard time hopping around a football field. The important thing is not to plan a game requiring abilities the participants don't have *or* a game that is so simple it seems boring and juvenile.

6. Dress. Many games demand more than normal stress on clothing. No game should require special or "official" clothing, but it is always important to warn people to wear "grubbies" or clothes that can take extra wear and tear. You can, of course, choose games that take into consideration how the people are dressed if they can't change.

7. Play space. Always keep in mind the amount of space you have in which to play. Take into account ceiling heights, wind, fences, playing surface, etc. In other words, don't plan a game like *Weather Balloon Volleyball* in an area like the beach where there is usually a fairly stiff wind (which causes the weather balloon to blow three blocks away and, therefore, tends to end the game prematurely.)

8. Time. Time is not really that important. As long as people are having fun, time limits and schedules are irrelevant. But it is important to recognize that time does have an effect. Don't

play too many games in a short time period or one game that lasts too long. Interrupt the game if the participants are bored or extend a game if everyone is enjoying it. *You control the time, don't let the time control you.*

9. Program. You should take into consideration what activity precedes and/or follows each game. If it is the first night of camp, plan maximum energy games that wear everyone out (to minimize late night hanky-panky). If there is a meeting after the games, don't conclude with games that result in wet clothing or clothing covered with egg.

10. Theme. Themes are usually corny, but once in a while you can adapt your games around a theme, such as "Bug Night" — events using VW's (VW Push, VW Stuff, VW Obstacle Course, etc.)

11. Weather. When planning an outdoor game event, never be caught unprepared. If it rains or snows, adapt the games to accommodate the bad weather or have an alternate indoor location planned. If you are planning a snow retreat in the mountains, be prepared in case there is no snow.

12. Equipment. Almost every game requires some kind of equipment. Of course, you always try to get the kind of equipment that will contribute to the best play possible. *But you are not a slave to equipment.* If you can't find a volleyball, then use a soccer ball, four square ball, or whatever else you can find. If what you find looks like it will affect the outcome of the game, then change the rules. We have played broom hockey with a volleyball, soccer ball, grapefruit (yes, grapefruit), two tee-shirts wadded up, etc.

13. Variety. Try to avoid playing too many similar games. Each game should provide a brand new way to have fun. Don't just play the "oldies but goodies." Get adventurous.

14. Purpose. By now you get the picture; the overall purpose of every game is to have fun. But beyond that, games can help achieve many different purposes such as wearing out restless campers on the last night, helping people to become better acquainted, or providing physical exercise. The point is

to choose games carefully and use them to accomplish your goals for the group.

Well, there you have it, the Fun-N-Games magic formula for effective gameplaying. Unfortunately, we can't guarantee they will all work. That's because games are for people and no two people experience games in exactly the same way. But *these guidelines will help*. So try them. If they don't work, then *you* can write the next Fun-N-Games book.

THE GAME EVENT

One of the best ways to use the games in this book is to incorporate them into what we call a "game event" — a full day or evening of games in a gymnasium or park, or an athletic field or beach. The object is always the same — to have lots of fun with everyone playing and enjoying the day.

Planning the Day

It is usually a good idea to start with easy games that go quickly, involve everyone, and "break the ice." Mixers make good starters because they not only require minimum skill (no problem of embarrassment), they also help people become better acquainted.

The rest of the games should be played in a sequence to minimize dead time between games and leave the players in position for the following game.

The last game to be played should be a real "rip-snorter" (recreation term) to conclude the event with a real climax.

Sample Indoor Game Event

Easy, fun opener	1. Barnyard
Puts groups into teams	
Mixer	2. John-john
	3. Clumps (or Tin Pan Bang Bang)
Elimination games	4. Balloon Stomp
(No teams needed)	5. Pull-up
Boys breather	6. King of the Circle (girls)
Girls breather	7. King of the Circle (Boys)

19

	8. Broom Twist Relay
	9. Inner Tube Relay
Four quick relays	10. Waddle Walk Relay
	11. Sock Tail Relay
Active, rough game	12. Broom Hockey
Teams seated	13. Indoor Scavenger Hunt
(breather)	14. Mad Ads
Wild finale	15. Snow Fight

Sample Outdoor Game Event

1. American Eagle

2. Run the Gauntlet

3. Tail Grab

4. Birdie on the Perch

5. Amoeba

6. Car Stuff

7. Polish Baseball

8. Pike's Peak

It is always a good idea to plan some breathers into a game event. This may be accomplished with games requiring little or no energy (Confusion, Coordination Clap, etc.). You could also use a skit, stunt, some group singing, or a refreshment break.

Pre-Game Preparations

Supervisors (referees): You will need several responsible people to help conduct and supervise the games, especially when large groups of people are involved. A good ratio should be about one leader for each twenty players. Make sure the "referees" are well identified with striped jerseys or fluorescent jackets. Be certain you and the referees understand the rules of the game thoroughly. Practice the game first with a test group to work out any bugs or situations not explained in the "rule book." If you have to read the rules, you are not familiar enough with the game.

Safety: Although all the games in *Fun-N-Games* are "low risk" games, there is still a risk, so appropriate safety precautions should be taken:

1. Have each participant bring a parent release form so that immediate care can be given those injured.

2. Have adequate first aid equipment on hand.

3. Arrange lists of doctors and hospitals close by with routes planned. Assign people ahead of time to drive, call parents, and get to medical equipment.

4. Double check your insurance coverage to make sure all injuries will be covered adequately.

If you notice that a game is getting too rough, stop the game and find ways to slow it down so that needless injury is avoided.

Although injuries may and do occur, don't be afraid to play a game because it seems rough or involves some risk. With proper safety measures and good supervision, serious injury can be avoided.

CREATIVE GAME PLAYING

Choosing Teams

If you use games requiring teams, don't make a big deal out of choosing them. Choosing teams takes too long and embarrasses those who have the misfortune of being last. The best option is to use a game like "Barnyard" that automatically puts everyone into groups that can be changed into teams before anyone realizes what has happened.

Most of the games in *Fun-N-Games* do not require the usual abilities, so the quality of a team is not determined by such things as size, strength, or athletic ability. Teams are important because they bring random groups of people together and help create community. So it just doesn't matter if teams are perfectly even or full of talent. A team simply needs to have a group of people *who want to play.*

Presentation of the Game

You must be able to explain the game simply, clearly, and as quickly as possible. If the rules and instructions of the game are not understood by everyone, the result may be mass confusion. That means you must have everyone's attention. *Never* try to shout directions over the noise of an inattentive group. For large groups, this may be solved by using a public address system or a "bullhorn." A good referee's whistle or marine boat horn (available in boat supply stores) may also come in handy. You might have a standing rule that whenever the horn or whistle goes off everyone must sit down right where he is and stop all talking and noise. The last person to do so gets a "penalty" (loss of points for team, water balloon, etc.). You don't have to enforce the rules too strictly, especially if the violator happens to be bigger than you!

Once you have the attention of the group, explain the game clearly and with enthusiasm. Make it sound fun. (The explanation should be as much fun as the game itself.)

If the game requires teams, you should have the teams chosen before you introduce the game so that you can get right into it after everyone knows how to play. This saves time and prevents confusion.

It is always a good idea to demonstrate the game to show exactly how the game is played. It is usually easier to *show* the group how to play than it is to *tell* them how. And, by the way, if the game gets started and it is obvious it is not being played correctly, then stop the game immediately and explain it again.

Playing the Game

When the game is in play, you should watch carefully to make sure everyone is getting into it and is having a good time. Don't insist on perfection or absolute precision in following the rules of the game. If the rules are being broken and need some enforcing, do it quickly and gently. Stay loose and let the game go wherever it leads, so long as everyone is having fun.

The best time to end a game that can go on indefinitely is just as soon as there are signs it might be going downhill. A game usually has a "peak," when everyone is enjoying it the most, and then it begins to slide. Don't let it get boring or tiring. Simply find a good way to end it. This may be done by announcing "one more minute to play" or "last round," etc. For this reason, it is advisable not to tell the groups ahead of time exactly how long the game will go. Leave it somewhat open-ended.

If a game is not going over at the outset, it should be stopped. Never insist that a game be continued when it is obvious the group does not like it. No matter how much planning and preparation you've done, stop and go on to something else.

Even with a great book like this one, it is still possible to pick a loser!

Another good time to quit is when the game is getting too lopsided — that is, when one team is slaughtering another. If there is no chance of getting the losing team back into the game, then it would be best to cut it off. If you can, however, you might try to find a way to even up a game while it is still in progress, if everyone agrees (add more players to the losing team or change the scoring procedure).

Controlling Team Competition

For games to be played effectively, there must always be a goal — an incentive for playing. Winning is a motivating reality that we all have to deal with, but we *can* make winning positive, fun, and beneficial to *all* concerned. We do that by insuring that the distance between the teams is close and that all teams have a chance to win right up to the last. There are a number of techniques to use:

Referees: There are two kinds of referees. First is the "Textbook Tyrant" type. He sees his role to impress all the "peons" playing with his technical expertise on all matters of rule trivia. It is his function to establish his authority on all matters of question and to insure a technically efficient game. He feels incompetent to referee unless he is wearing his official referee outfit. If you end up with a referee like this, you have a couple of options. 1. Ask him to commit hari-kari. 2. You commit hari-kari. 3. Cancel the game.

"Smooth Sam" is there to help the game run smoothly and simply. He understands that rules were invented to help people enjoy a game, not fight over trivia. This kind of referee understands that an "infraction" occurs when people's enjoyment of the game is in jeopardy. So if one team is desperately behind, he becomes more observant of the "winning" team and less observant of the team that is behind. This usually results in a balancing of the score so that everyone can then have fun again.

Points: Many groups use points to tabulate the standings of team competition throughout the period of competition. Give lots of points. Points are free, so don't be stingy by giving ten, fifty or even a hundred points for placement. Give them a thousand points, three thousand points!!! After all, who wants to play hard for fifty measly points when he can win *three thousand*. Keep the point spread extremely close by giving every place points (including last) and keeping the amounts between places small. For example:

1st — 3000
2nd — 2900
3rd — 2800
4th — 2700
5th — 2600

As you can see, the last place team actually only has 400 points between them and first. A team could lose every event and still be within striking distance.

Variety: There are team games in which all teams compete *at the same time* and there are team games in which teams compete *one at a time*. By interspersing one-at-a-time games among the others, you can help even up the competition between teams. When you have team competition a team at a time, *always have the team currently ahead in the standings go first*. The teams following have time to learn from the others mistakes and almost always the first team of the event does not win.

If you are running an event for more than one day, increase the number of events on the last day so that, in effect, a team in last place could make an amazing comeback and end up in first place.

Be sure to vary the skills required in each event so that no one group can dominate the competition.

TEAM GAMES

TEAM GAMES

A-B-C's

This game is good for large groups of 40 or more. Divide into teams. The leader must locate himself high above the players, up on a roof, hill, or other high place, so that he can see everyone below. He then yells out a letter of the alphabet, and each team must form that letter on the field as quickly as possible (as a marching band would do). The first team to form the letter wins. In case of a tie, teams may also be judged for the best job of forming the letter.

AMOEBA

Divide into teams and simply tie a rope around the team at their waists. To do this, have the team bunch up together as closely as they can, and hold their hands up in the air while you tie the rope around them. After they are tied, they can race to a goal and back. Unless they work together and cooperate as a team, they will go nowhere. This is a fun game for camps and outdoor activities.

BALLOON BASKETBALL

Arrange your chairs in the following manner. There should be an equal number of people on each of the two teams. One team faces in one direction, the second team faces the other direction. There can be any number of players on a team, just

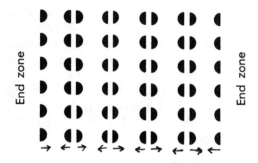

so long as the teams are equal. The two rows of chairs on each end should face inward.

After all the players are seated in their team's chairs, toss a balloon into the center of the players. The players cannot stand, but they must try to "bat" the balloon to the end zone they are facing, using only their hands. As soon as the balloon drops into the end zone over the heads of the last row of people, the team going in that direction wins 2 points. If the balloon goes out of bounds, just throw it back into the center. Play can be to 20 points, or it may end after 15 minutes of play.

BARREL OF FUN

Line up two teams. Each is given a 55-gallon drum with one side removed. Have each team pair off in twos (players about the same size). One person goes inside the barrel and the other pushes. When the signal is given, the one in the barrel changes places with the pusher. The first team to get its team through wins. If possible, the barrel should have two garage door handles welded or bolted inside it. This will give the person inside something with which to brace himself. It also keeps the tall people from being mangled.

BASKETBALL DERBY

Play a game of basketball on roller skates. It is extremely funny to watch as well as play. There is no out-of-bounds or dribbling, but the other regular rules apply. Other games (such as softball, football, etc.) may be played on roller skates as well with excellent results.

BASKETBALL PASS

This is a simple relay game in which two teams line up single file in two lines. Each team must have an equal number of players. At the front of each line, a basketball (or several basketballs) is given to the first player. He passes it to the player behind him by passing it *over his head*. The next one passes it *between his legs* to the one behind him and so on. The ball(s) continue to the end of the line going over and under, and the team who finishes first wins.

BEACH BALL PICKUP

Divide into teams. Teams then number off and line up opposite each other about twenty feet or so apart. Between the two teams, six beach balls (light ones) are placed on the floor. Two numbers are called and the two players on each team with those numbers begin play. Each pair must pick up three balls without using their hands or arms. If they drop a ball, they must start over. All three balls must be held between the two players and must be off the ground. The first pair to succeed is the winner. Repeat by calling two new numbers, and so on.

BLANKET PULL

Two teams are identically numbered and line up facing each

other. A blanket is placed in the center. A number is called and both people try to pull the blanket over their own goal.

BLIND MATE

Select three couples to compete in this simple game. One at a time, each couple is blindfolded and then separated by a distance of twenty feet or so. The pair must then walk toward each other, locate the other person, and hold hands. The couple to do it in the shortest time is the winner. To really make this tough, turn the players around a few times before they begin.

BLIND TAG

Conjure up something with a circumference of about twenty feet, such as two tables pushed together or rope wrapped around four chairs. Blindfold two people and put them on opposite sides of this object. Both must always be touching it. Designate one to be "it" and have the bystanders shout to their favorite which way to go to catch or avoid being caught by the other. Beware of high-speed collisions. One variation is to remove one of the two contestants and let everyone shout directions to the unsuspecting victim. Another is to have everyone remain silent and let the players listen for each other. This won't work on a carpet.

BLIND VOLLEYBALL

Divide the players into two equal groups. The two teams then get on each side of a volleyball court and sit down either on chairs or on the floor in rows, as in regular volleyball. The "net" should be a solid divider that obstructs the view of the other team, such as blankets hung over a regular volleyball net or rope. The divider should also be low enough that players cannot see under it. Then play volleyball. Use a big, light plastic ball instead of a volleyball. Regular volleyball rules and boundaries apply. A player may not stand up to hit the ball. The added dimension of the solid net adds a real surprise element to the game when the ball comes flying over the net.

BLOODY MARSHMALLOW

Have the players pair off. Partners stand about ten feet apart

facing each other. Each gets five marshmallows and a paper
cup full of catsup. One at a time, each person dips a marshmallow in the catsup and tries to toss it in his partner's mouth. The
partner tries to catch it in his mouth. The couple that catches
the most out of all ten marshmallows, wins.

BROOM HOCKEY

This game may be played with as many as 30 or as few as 5 per
team, but only 5 or 6 are actually on the field at one time from
each team. Two teams compete by (at a whistle) running out
onto the field, grabbing their brooms and swatting a volleyball
placed in the center through the opposite goal. Each team has a
"goalie," as in ice hockey or soccer, who can grab the ball with
his hands and throw it back onto the playing field. If the ball
goes out of bounds, the referee throws it back in. The ball may
not be touched with hands, or kicked; but only hit with the
broom. Score 1 point for each time ball passes between goal
markers.

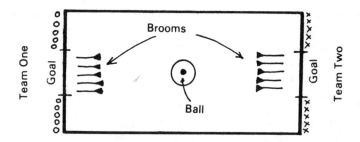

For a team with 30 members, for example, have them number
off by sixes, which would give you 6 teams of 5 members each.
Let all the "ones" play a 3 minute period, then the "twos," etc.

BUCKET BRIGADE

Each team lines up single file with a bucket of water on one
end and an empty bucket on the other. Each team member has
a paper cup. The object of the game is to transfer the water
from one bucket to the other by pouring the water from cup to
cup down the line. First team to get all the water to the empty
bucket wins.

BY THE "SEAT OF YOUR PANTS" VOLLEYBALL

This can be an excellent indoor game for large groups, especially during rainy weather. Divide the group into two teams. Set up a volleyball net so that top of net is approximately five feet above the floor. Each player is instructed to sit down on his team's side of the net so that his legs are crossed in front of him. From this position a regular game of volleyball is played with the following changes:

1. Use a "light" beach ball type ball (or a "nerf" ball).

2. Use hands and head only (no feet).

3. All serves must be made from center of group, and overhand.

Rotation would look something like this:

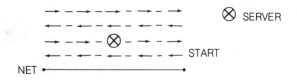

4. Because of limited mobility of each player a larger number of participants is suggested (20-25 per team).

5. All other rules of volleyball prevail.

CANDY RACE

Tie a piece of candy onto the middle of a length of string and have two players on each end of the string, with the string held in their teeth. On a signal, they chew the string toward the candy, and the first to reach the candy and get it into his mouth wins. No hands are allowed.

CANNED LAUGHTER

Bring plenty of empty soft drink cans to the meeting and have three or more players compete to see who can stack them the highest within a given time limit. The winner may be awarded a six-pack of his favorite pop.

CAPTURE THE FLAG

The playing field needs to look like this:

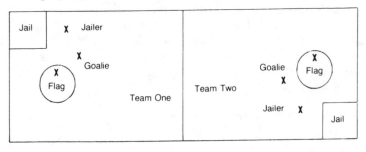

Team 1 is on one side of the field, and Team 2 is on the other side. The idea of the game is to somehow capture the flag, located in the other team's territory, without getting tagged. (Or tackled, clobbered, etc.) Once you cross over the line in the middle of the field, you can be tagged, and sent to "jail" which is set up behind each team back by the flag. However, if you are in jail, one of your teammates can free you by getting to the jail without getting tagged, and then he can tag you, which frees you. You both get a free walk back to safety. Each team gets one "goalie" who watches the flag from a distance of about ten feet away, and also a "jailer," who guards the jail. The idea is to work out some strategy with your teammates to rush the flag, or in some other way, "capture the flag."

CAPTURE THE FOOTBALL

This, of course, is based on capture the flag — however, it may be played by smaller groups with less room as well as large groups. Also, it doesn't have to be completely dark. Instead of using flags — use footballs. These are placed on each team's territory. You must get the other team's football over to your team's territory. You may pass the ball over the line to win, or run it over. If you are tagged, you must remain a prisoner until a teammate tags you. If you pass the ball to a teammate over the line which separates the team territories and your teammate drops it — you both become prisoners. If the "pass" is "complete," your team wins. You must adapt the capture the flag rules to your group and setting for the best results.

CAR STUFF

For this *wild* game, you need an old car that won't be hurt by a little dent or some dirt. Players line up on one side of the car (with both front or back doors open) and on a signal, run through the car, in one side and out the other. After going through the car, the players return to the end of the line and run through again until the time limit is up. Each team has a "timer" and a "counter," and the object is to see how many players can be run through the car in the time limit (one minute, two minutes, etc.). Each team gets a try. To play this game without using a car, use a large cardboard box, a bench that the players must crawl under, or simply have three players stand in a row with their legs spread, and the team must crawl under their legs.

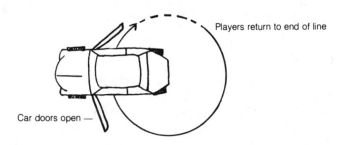

Players return to end of line

Car doors open —

CREEPER RACE

Get several mechanic's creepers (the type used by mechanics under cars). Line teams up and have races. Players lie on the creepers and race by propelling with hands only, feet only, on their backs, etc. This is best on cement floors.

CATCH THE WIND

Have one person lie on the floor with a straw in his mouth. At his head, place a chair. A second person sits in the chair facing the person on the floor and has a party blower in his mouth. The chair back should be toward the person on the floor and the seated person should rest his chin on the chair back. A third person sits next to the person on the floor and places Kleenex (or any other brand) tissues one at a time on the end of the straw. The person on the floor then blows the tissue up in the air and the person in the chair tries to catch it with the party blower. This game requires three-person teams, obviously, and the winning team is the first to successfully catch a given number of tissues. The distance from the blower on the floor to the catcher may vary depending on the distance up that people can blow.

CHARIOT RACES

This game is best played in a gymnasium, or anywhere there is a nice slick floor. Set up a circular "track" and have boys (horses) pull girls (charioteers) on blankets (chariots). There should be two fellows pulling and one girl riding. Make sure she is prepared to hold on tightly, as the rider normally is thrown off the blanket going around curves unless the team works together to prevent that. First team to complete three laps is the winner.

CHINESE PING-PONG

About ten or so people stand around a Ping-Pong table, one on each end, the rest on the sides. The first person serves the ball over the net to the one on the other end just as in regular Ping-Pong, but after he serves it, he puts the paddle down on the table (with the handle sticking over the edge) and gets in the line to his left. The next person in line (to the server's right) picks up the paddle and waits for the ball to be returned. The line keeps rotating around the table in a clockwise fashion, with each person hitting the ball once from whichever end of the table he happens to be. If he drops the paddle, misses the ball, or hits it off the table, he is eliminated. When it gets down to the last two people, they must hit the ball, put the paddle down, turn around, then pick up the paddle and hit the ball. Last one remaining wins.

CIRCLE SOCCER

Two teams get into one circle, half on one side and half on the other.

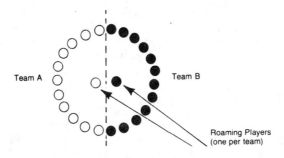

A ball is thrown into the circle and the players try to kick it out through the other team's side. If the ball is kicked out over the heads of the players, the point goes to the nonkicking team. If the ball is kicked out below the heads of the players, the kicking team gets the point. Hands may not be used at all, only feet and bodies. No one may move out of position except one player per team who may kick the ball to his teammates if the ball gets stuck in the center. He may not score, however, or cross into the other team's territory. If the roaming player gets hit with the ball (when kicked by the other team), the kicking team gets a point.

CLOTHES PUT ON

Have a group of gals at one end of the room and a group of boys at the other. The girls are given boys clothes to put on over their own and the boys are given girls' clothes. The first group to have on every piece of clothing wins.

CLOTHESPIN CHALLENGE

Two contestants are selected and seated in chairs facing each other with their knees touching. Each is shown a large pile of clothespins at the right of their chairs. Each is blindfolded and given two minutes to pin as many clothespins as possible on the pant legs of the other contestant.

CONTEST OF THE WINDS

Draw a large square on the floor and divide it into four equal parts, designated as the North, East, South and West. Divide the group into four teams designated by the same names.

Scatter dried leaves or cotton balls evenly in each quarter of the square. At a given signal, the "winds begin to blow" and each team tries to *blow* (no hands allowed) the leaves out of its square into another. Set a time limit and the team with the least leaves (or cotton balls) in its square wins.

CORN SHUCKING RACE

For this little game, you will need several ears of corn. Select three or more volunteers to try and "shuck" an ear of corn using only their bare feet. No hands are allowed. Whoever finishes first, or whoever has done the best job within a given time limit is the winner. Award an appropriate prize, such as a bag of corn chips.

COTTON BALLS

Have a guy volunteer to see how fast he can pick up cotton balls with a spoon and place them in a bowl. Blindfold him, give him a spoon, and have him stand behind a table with a bowl on it. Around the bowl, sprinkle a dozen or so cotton balls. (Let the volunteer see them.) After he is blindfolded, remove the cotton balls. Make sure he only uses one hand.

CRAB BALL

This is an active game for groups of twenty or more. All that is needed is a playground ball. Divide into four teams of equal size, and form a square with each team forming one side of the square. Players should then sit down on the floor, and number off from one to however many players are on each team. To begin the game the leader places the ball in the center and calls a number. All four persons of that number "crab walk" out to the ball. "Crab Walking" is bending over backwards and then walking on all fours. The object is to kick the ball over the heads of one of the other teams (other than one's own). When a crab walker succeeds in kicking it over the heads of another team, the team over whose head it went, gets a point. The remaining members of the team must stay in place with their seats on the floor. They may block the balls coming at them either by kicking, using their bodies, or using their heads. They may never use their hands or arms. They also may try to kick it over the heads of an opposing team. Either way, the team over whose head the ball goes gets the point. When the first team reaches ten points, the game is ended and the *lowest* score wins.

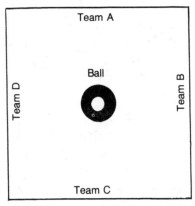

CRAZY BASKETBALL

Divide your entire group into two teams with any number of players. The game is played on a regular basketball court, but without regular basketball rules. In this game, anything goes. The object is to score the most baskets any way you can. You can run, pass, dribble, or throw the basketball with no restrictions. All that matters is to make a basket. Players can ride piggy-back for height. This game works best with 50 to 200 participants.

CROSSWORD PEOPLE

Divide the group into teams of equal size (12 to 24 on a team). Prepare ahead of time sets of letters of the alphabet on 12"x12" cards that each team member hangs around his neck. Each team should have identical sets of letters, consisting of frequently used vowels and consonants, plus two or three rarely used letters such as Q, X, or Z. At a signal each team tries to form a "crossword" puzzle, using as many of the team as possible, within a given time limit. Each team should have a captain who directs his team and keeps order. For example, using the letters PGOFYECA JAXOTIIUM, a team could line up this way:

```
            JUMPING
              I      O
           TAX      O
              CAFE
                    Y
```

Award points for the team using the most of its team, the longest word, the most words, etc. Another idea would be to assign point value to each letter and add up points as if you were playing the game "Scrabble."

CROQUET-GOLF

This is actually miniature golf played with a croquet set. Wickets are used instead of cups in the ground. Set up your own nine-hole course by arranging the wickets around the yard. Tag each wicket with the hole number as well as placing small signs at each tee where the players must begin each hole. Determine how many strokes will be par for each hole and indicate this on the tee sign along with the hole number. Try to make each hole different by having to go around objects such a shrubs, through tin cans and tires, and up ramps and hills. Some croquet sets include wicket tags and tee signs for playing croquet-golf.

CROSBEE

This game is a mixture of Frisbee and LaCrosse. All that is needed is a playing field, a Frisbee, and from ten to seventy-five players. Goals are set up on opposite ends of the field, two markers about ten feet apart. Divide up into two teams. Each team selects goalies, and perhaps other positions such as defense, offense, forward, middle, back, etc. The two teams then line up on opposite ends of the field and the Frisbee is placed in the middle. On the starting whistle, players run for the Frisbee, and the first to get it may pass it to any other player on his team. When a player catches it, he may run with it, pass it, or down it, which is a "stop." (To down it, he simply falls on it.) Any player carrying the Frisbee may be "tagged" by a member of the other team and must then surrender the Frisbee to him immediately. (Referees should make judgments on this.) If a player downs the Frisbee before being tagged, he can then stand up and throw it to any other player on his team without interference. However, once the Frisbee is thrown, it may be intercepted. Also, a person downing the Frisbee cannot score after downing it. Goals are scored by throwing the Frisbee between the goal markers.

CROWS AND CRANES

Divide the group into two teams. One side is the "Crows," the other is the "Cranes." The two teams are lined up facing each other on two lines four or five feet apart. The leader flips a coin (heads — "Crows," tails — "Cranes") and yells out the name of the team which won the toss. If he yells "Crows," the "crows" must turn around and run, with the "Cranes" in hot pursuit. If any of the "Cranes" succeed in touching a member (or members) of the "Crows" before he crosses a given line (20 to 60 feet away), he is considered a captive of the "Cranes" and must aid the "Cranes" when play continues. The team which captures all the members of the other team is the winner.

CUT THE CAKE

Pack flour in big bowl and turn upside down on TV tray or baking sheet. It is a mold now; put cherry on top. Everyone in circle around cake must cut off some part (be it large or small) of the cake and then the knife is passed around the circle. The more the cake is cut, the closer you get to the cherry in the center. Whoever cuts the cake, causing the cherry to "fall" has to pick it up with his teeth with hands behind his back, and eat the cherry.

DARK DRAW

Everyone in the group is given a sheet of paper and pen. Players are given five minutes (or more) to draw anything they want. But . . . lights are all turned out during the time of drawing their picture. Pictures judged and winner given prize.

DART BOARD BLAST

Make a dart board out of cardboard or acoustical tile and hang it on the wall. Players bring pictures of themselves or each other and glue them on. These "targets" are a good way to take out frustrations. This could also be a good way to select a "volunteer" for something. Have someone throw a dart onto the board with all the pictures on it. Whoever gets hit "volunteers."

DING BALL

This game is played in a swimming pool with a volley ball net dividing two teams. The teams are given every possible kind of ball (ping pong, volley, football, soccer, beach ball, etc.). The object is to throw as many balls as possible over the net so that the opposing team has the most balls on its side when the whistle blows. It's a silly game, but it catches on fast.

"DO IT ON PAPER" SHUFFLE

This is a relay game in which each person is given two pieces of paper (newspaper works fine). They are to go between two points stepping only on paper. They step on the paper in front of them, then turn around and pick up the one behind them, place it in front of them, step on it, and turn around and pick up the paper behind them, repeating this action until they reach the designated point. Team completing the race first is the winner.

DR. TANGLE

Have a group of any number of people hold hands. Have one person leave the room. Start in a circle, then without breaking hands, go under and over other people's arms. When the group is all knotted up, call the person back into the room and have him try to untangle the group without breaking hands.

DRIVING THE PIGS TO MARKET

The teams are lined up behind the starting line. Give the first player a three-foot stick, yardstick, or broom handle, and a "pig" in the form of a coke bottle or egg. At the signal "go" the first player drives the pig to the goal and back by pushing with wands. The second player does the same until all have run.

EGG ROLL

In this relay, contestants roll a raw egg along an obstacle course with their noses. If the egg breaks, the player must start over with a fresh egg.

EGG TOSS

Three couples line up with the partners facing each other about three feet apart. Each couple is given an egg. They toss the egg back and forth, each time taking one step backward. The couple who can keep the egg from breaking the longest is the winner. Water balloons may also be used instead of eggs.

ESKINOSE

Teams line up, alternating by sex, boy-girl-boy-girl, etc. One person on the end of each line gets a lipstick smear on the end of his (or her) nose. The idea is to see how far down the line you can pass the lipstick smear by rubbing noses. The team to get it the farthest, or the team to get it the farthest in the time limit (30 seconds) wins.

EXCEDRIN WAMP

Have each boy (4 to 6 — or as many as 100 to 300) put a paper bag loosely over his head down to his ears. Each boy has a rolled-up newspaper. The object is to knock the other guy's "hat" off without losing one's own. No one is allowed to hold his hat on.

EXPANDABLE HOPSCOTCH

This is a grown-up version of the old child's game of hopscotch. Secure small size carpet remnants from any carpet store (they usually charge 10 - 25¢ for each one). These are the hopscotch squares. The game is played as usual, except that the squares are spaced further and further apart as the game progresses until the players are jumping several feet between squares. It's good competition and is great for laughs.

FAN THE BALLOON

Each team gets a balloon and a fan (which can be anything

such as a record album cover). On the signal, each player on the team must fan the balloon, without touching it, around a goal and back. Balloon also may not touch the floor.

FEET-BALL

This is a good indoor game which is very active and requires real teamwork. Divide the group into two teams and seat them (in chairs) in two lines, facing each other. The object is for the teams to move the ball (a volleyball) toward and through their goal (at the end of the line) by using only their feet. Players must keep their arms behind the chairs to keep from touching the ball, which is a penalty. To begin the game, drop the ball between the two teams in the middle. The game may last any length of time desired. To avoid injuries to feet, shoes should be removed. Also, make sure the two teams are just far enough apart that their feet barely touch when legs are extended on both sides.

FLAMINGO FOOTBALL

Announce that you are going to play "tackle football, boys against the girls!" The guys usually get pretty charged up about that idea. Then announce that the rules are the same as regular tackle football, except for one thing. The boys must hold one foot up off the ground with one hand at all times. They must run, pass, hike, catch, and even kick on one foot. The girls usually clobber the guys with this one.

FLOURED LIFESAVERS

Fill two pie tins or pans with flour. Drop several lifesavers in each and mix them in so they are not visible. Have two players race to see who can retrieve the most lifesavers out of the flour in one minute.

FOOT PAINTING

Choose a group of boys (number of boys should be one-half the number of letters in the name of your group or organization). They all sit down in a line facing audience. You paint the letters in the name of your group on the bottom of their feet (jumbled up) with a felt marker or poster paint. At a signal, they are to try and get the letters unscrambled and in order (read-able) without any of them getting up or moving from their positions.

FOOT WRESTLING

This is just like Indian Arm wrestling, only you have players sit on the floor, lock toes, and then at a given signal, try to pin the other person's foot on the floor.

FORTY-INCH DASH

Give three players a forty-inch piece of string with a marshmallow tied to one end of it. On a signal, each person puts the loose end of the string in his mouth and, without using his hands, "eats" his way to the marshmallow. The first person to reach the marshmallow is the winner.

FOUR-LETTER WORD

Every member of the group has a large letter of the alphabet pinned on. At the signal each person tries to find three others with whom he can form a four-letter word within a one-minute time limit. Those failing to form a word are out, and the game continues until everyone is eliminated.

FOUR SQUARE

A sixteen- to twenty-foot square is drawn on the floor.

Four players stand in boxes 1 through 4 and the remaining players line up outside #4. Player #1 is always the server. He hits the ball underhand to one of the other squares after first bouncing it in his own square once. The receiver then tries to keep it in play after it has bounced once in his square by hitting it underhand to a square other than to the one from which he received it. Play continues after each serve until someone commits one of the following fouls:

   a. Failing to return the ball after it bounces once.

   b. Hitting the ball out of the square.

   c. Hitting the ball back to the person who hit it to him.

   d. Hitting the ball with the fist or downhanded.

   e. Stepping over the server's line on a serve.

   f. Playing in someone else's square.

   g. Allowing the ball to touch body (other than the hands).

   h. Holding the ball.

The person who commits the foul leaves the game and lines up in back of the line (square 4). All players move up. The object is to get into server's square and stay there as long as possible.

EGG BLOW

Obtain about three to four feet of clear plastic tubing (surgical tubing) or hose, and by tapping two small holes in the opposite ends of an egg, you can insert the insides of the egg into the tubing. After you get the egg inside the tubing, have two players who are real "blowhards" get on each end of the tubing, and at a given signal begin to blow on their end of the tubing. Object is to keep the egg away from your side, and blast the other guy with it.

FRISBEE GOLF

Lay out a short golf course around the area using telephone poles, light posts, fence posts, tree trunks, etc. for "holes." You can set up places as the tees or designate a certain distance from the previous "hole" (such as ten feet) for the starting place. Each person needs a Frisbee. The object of the game is to take as few throws as possible to hit all the "holes." Each person takes his first throw from the tee and then stands where it landed for his next throw until he hits the "hole." Of course, discretion must be used when the Frisbee lands in a bush or tree. One penalty "throw" is added to the score if the Frisbee can't be thrown from where it lands. The course may be as simple or as complicated as the skill of the participants warrants. Such things as doglegs, doorways, arches, and narrow fairways add to the fun of the course. Take three or four good Frisbee throwers through the course to set the par for each hole. It is a good test of skill, but anyone can do it. Two other games for a "Frisbee Night" could include a *distance throw* and an *accuracy throw* (like through a hula hoop from thirty feet).

FRISBEE RELAY

Divide the group into equal teams of 5 or 6 per team. Any number of teams may play at once. Each team will need a frisbee. The playing area should have plenty of length, such as a road (without traffic) or a large open field. Each team should spread out in a line with players about 50 feet apart or so. The first person throws the frisbee to the second, who allows the frisbee to land. That person then stands where the frisbee landed and throws it toward the third person, who throws it to the fourth, and so on. The object is to see which team can throw it the greatest distance in the shortest time. Award points for throwing it the farthest, and points for finishing first. For added fun, have the men throw left-handed (or right-handed if they are left-handed). Footballs may be substituted for frisbees if they are easier to get.

GIANT JIGSAW PUZZLE

Obtain an outdoor billboard sign from a sign company (they come rolled up and easy to carry), and cut it into a giant jigsaw puzzle. Use it as a game to see which team can put it together first.

GIANT PUSHBALL

It is possible to purchase a "giant pushball" from various sporting goods stores or sporting goods supply houses. The ball is approximately 6 feet in diameter and weighs 30 to 40 pounds. It is great for camps and other special activities. Normally the ball is covered with canvas, and is guaranteed for life.

A typical pushball game is as follows: Teams line up on either side of an open field. The ball is placed in the middle. On a signal, the two teams (which may consist of any number) try to push the ball through their team's goal on one end of the field. Four teams may play, and have goals on all four sides of the field. The goal may be the entire length of the side of the field. It is really a wild game. For best results, the ball should be pushed upward and over the heads of opposing players.

GIANT SLIP 'N' SLIDE

A giant "slip 'n' slide" may be made from a large piece of heavy plastic. Station players at intervals around edge to hold it in place. Give the kids a grassy lawn, plenty of garden hose, and they will have a blast. Have contests to see who can slide the farthest standing up, lying on his stomach, or his back, and sitting down.

GIANT VOLLEYBALL

Two teams of any number can play this funny volleyball game which uses a giant weather balloon for a ball. Six to eight feet in diameter, the balloon is inflated with a vacuum cleaner. The entire team gets under the ball and pushes it over the net. The opposing team returns it. Giant weather balloons are available from Army surplus stores for about $3.00 each.

GIRLS TIRE CHANGE

This is a great game for outdoor activities. Two (or more) groups of girls each get a car, a spare tire, a jack, tire iron, etc., and race to see which group can change a tire the fastest. For added excitement, after the tire is changed they must push the car a certain distance across a finish line.

GLOVE-MILKING CONTEST

Fill two rubber gloves with milk. Punch pin holes in the ends of the fingers and hang them from a stick held over two buckets. Two players then attempt to "milk" the gloves. Whoever gets the most milk into the bucket within the time limit wins.

GRAPE TOSS

Teams appoint one player who is the "tosser." He gets a bag of grapes. The rest of the team gets in a circle around him. The tosser is in the middle. He must toss grapes to everyone on his team, one at a time, and each team member must catch the grape in his or her mouth. The first team to go around its circle (the whole team), wins.

HAPPY BIRTHDAY RACE

Divide the group into teams. On a signal, each team must line up according to date of birth, with the youngest person on one end of the line, and the oldest on the other. Any team out of order after the time limit (or the last team to get in the correct order) loses.

HULA HOOP PACK

Each team tries to see how many people they can get inside a hula hoop. Naturally it is best to have your larger players doing the packing with the smaller ones getting packed in. If a genuine "hula hoop" is not available, then any strong hoop will work, or a thick rope tied into a circle will work also. Note: If your group like to pack themselves into things, try packing a phone booth, or a Volkswagen, or a bathtub, or a tractor tire, or anything else you can think of.

HUMAN OBSTACLE COURSE

Each team stands in single file behind a line. Ten additional team members are used as obstacles: pole to circle around, leg tunnel to go under, kneelers to leap over, sitters with outstretched legs to step in and among, then another pole. On signal, first person in line goes completely around pole, under tunnel, over kneelers, in and among sitters (not missing any stepping space), around pole then runs back. Next person goes, etc. If an obstacle is missed or improperly executed, the runner must repeat that obstacle.

HUMAN SCRABBLE

Divide group into teams. Distribute cards at random which

have a letter of the alphabet written on them. On a signal, each team must use the letters which they have and form the longest word they possibly can. The longest word wins. Mix all the letter cards up again, re-distribute them and play several rounds. Each round has a thirty-second time limit. Be sure to include plenty of common letters (especially vowels). For a variation of this game, see the game "Crossword People."

HUMAN WHEELBARROW

This is a relay game in which the boys must walk on their hands while their feet are being held by their partner, boy or girl. Contestants must maneuver through an obstacle course of some kind.

HUNTERS AND HOUNDS

Players pair off, one being the "hunter" and the other being the "hound." The hunters each get a shoebox (or similar box) and the hounds try to go out and find (for the hunters) peanuts which have been hidden beforehand around the room. When a hound finds a peanut, he cannot touch it, but begins to howl, and his corresponding hunter comes and retrieves the peanut. When two or more hounds find the same peanut, each howls and the hunter who gets there first gets the nut. All hunters stay in a "lodge," a circle or specified area where they wait for their hounds to howl.

ICE CUBE RACE

Secure large blocks of ice (ice house) and get the Police Department to cordon off some streets. Have different ages compete against each other, pushing ice blocks up street. Works best on real hot days (so the ice melts faster). The object is to see how far you can push the ice before it is all melted.

ICE-MELTING CONTEST

Each team is given a 25-pound block of ice. Each ice block is weighed in, and the teams are given 10 minutes to try and melt as much of it as possible. No water, fire, crushing, or chipping of the ice is allowed. At the end of 10 minutes, each block is weighed again, and the block that lost the most weight wins.

INDOOR OLYMPICS

Below are several simple games suitable for an "Indoor Olympics." With a little creativity, you can add many more similar games to the list for a very exciting time.

Discus Throw: Paper plates are thrown for distance. Plates must be held like a discus. Each contestant takes two hops and a step, then throws the plate as far as he can.

Hammer Throw: Each contestant throws an inflated paper sack tied onto a 30-inch piece of string. Holding the loose end of the string, each contestant swings the sack around his head several times before throwing for distance.

Javelin Throw: Contestants throw toothpicks like javelins. With the throwing arm back, and the other arm out in front for balance, each contestant takes three running steps and throws the toothpick as far as possible. Knitting needles may also be used.

INNER TUBE SOCCER

This is a game of soccer, using the usual rules of the game, only subsituting an inner tube (automobile tire tube) for a normal soccer-style kickball. It really gives the game a new dimension. The tube should lie flat, and the playing surface should be relatively flat and smooth.

KICKBALL

The group is divided into two teams. Each team numbers off consecutively so that for every number on one team, there is a corresponding number on the opposite team. The teams line up facing each other, but in opposite order; i.e., the number "ones" of each team are at opposite ends of the line. A beach ball is used in the game with junior highers and a volley ball with senior highers or older. The ball is placed in the middle of the floor. When the player's number is called, the players from each team run and try to kick the ball through or over the opposing team line. They may use only their feet. The team members, standing on the line, may block with their hands, but may not otherwise use them.

KING OF THE GOATS

Choose a "Goat" from the group or one from each team and have them removed while the groups are given instruction. One group, "the crowd," is instructed to stand on the sidelines and shout instructions to the goat while the other group is told to form a circle holding hands. The goat is to be put in the center of the circle blindfolded. On signal the goat is to start chasing the circle and the circle is to move as a whole to avoid being caught. When the goat is ready to start, the circle group is instructed in his presence, to move silently and to make no sound and that the goat is to listen to the sideline crowd for his instructions as to which direction to go to catch the circle. As soon as the start signal is given the crowd starts to shout instructions to the goat: Go to the right, the left, now go back, go back, straight ahead, etc. The minute the game gets under way, the circle team, which had been so instructed before the goat arrived, immediately disbands and joins the crowd, leaving the goat an empty field. Let it run for a short time or until the goat guesses what is going on.

KING OF THE MOUNTAIN

Divide up into teams (schools, classes, etc.) and give each team a flag they are to try to plant on top of a hill. Of course, this must be done somewhere like at a camp where there is a suitable hill or mountain to climb. Award points for first, second, third, etc. places, plus points for just getting to the top among the first 10 or so kids.

KLEENEX BLOW

Divide the group into teams. Each team then receives a Kleenex (or any other brand) tissue and must keep the tissue in the air by blowing, and without touching it. Time each team, and the team able to keep the tissue up in the air the longest is the winner.

LAWN SKIING

For those who long for the mountain slopes or whose lakes and rivers may be dry, try this. Acquire several pairs of water skis and remove the fins from the undersides. Get the necessary number of tow ropes or just plain rope (you'll need at least 40 feet), and begin your races. Local school or park lawns (just watered) provide a slick surface and kids pulling the ropes provide the power. Many variations are possible using slalom skis, skim boards, inner tubes, etc. Other surfaces besides grass are suitable. Events may range from slaloms to marathons.

LEMONADE EATING CONTEST

Get three guys to participate in a lemonade eating contest. The idea is that instead of mixing the lemonade first, the contestants will eat the ingredients, and it will mix on its own. They must first drink a large glass of water, eat a raw lemon, followed by a tablespoon of sugar. First guy to finish wins.

LIPSTICK MASH

Using as many couples as you want, have the boys hold a tube of bright red lipstick in their mouths and attempt to apply it to the lips of their girl partners. The time limit is thirty seconds. When finished, the audience judges who did best.

LONGJOHN STUFF

Select two girls and have them put on a pair of long underwear (preferably the kind that have the "trapdoor" in back). The girls should be wearing pants under them. Throw some balloons out into the audience and have the group blow up the balloons and tie them, then bat them up to the front. You will probably need a hundred or so balloons, depending on the size of the balloons. On a signal, two girl assistants begin stuffing the balloons into each of the other girls' longjohns. The balloons should be stuffed in the legs, the arms, and all over. The idea is to see which girl can get the most balloons in the longjohns in two minutes, so they have to work fast. At the end of the time period, have the girls count the balloons by popping them (while they are still in the longjohns) with a pin.

MAD ADS

Each team receives a magazine (same one for all teams) and appoints a "runner." The leader then calls out a description of an ad somewhere in the magazine. The first team to tear the ad out of the magazine, give it to the runner, and have the runner give it to the leader, wins. The team with the most "wins" is the victor.

MATCHBOX RACE

This is a relay game in which players pass a matchbox cover (small wooden type match) down a row of people, from nose to nose without using hands.

MATH SCRAMBLE

Divide into teams. Each person is given a number on a piece of paper which is to be worn. (Numbers should begin at 0 and go up to 10 or the number of players on the team.) The leader stands an equal distance away from each team and yells out a "math problem" such as "2 times 8 minus 4 divided by 3" and the team must send the person with the correct answer (the person wearing the number "4" in this case) to the leader. No talking is allowed on the team. The correct person must simply get up and run. The first correct answer to get to the leader wins 100 points. The first team to reach 1,000 (or whatever) wins.

MATTRESS RACE

This is a relay game in which the male members of the teams carry all the girl members on their teams (one at a time) a distance of 100 feet from the starting point across the finish line on a mattress. The mattress must be carried shoulder high, or the group has to start over. The first team to get all their girls across the finish line is the winner.

MONKEY SOCCER

For a fast-action outdoor game, designate a rectangular area of grass as a "monkey soccer" field, with a width of at least three feet per player. Divide the group into two teams, and provide one ball, volleyball size, but quite a light weight.

Here are the rules:

1. The object of each play is for the team which has the ball to get it across the other team's end of the court.

2. However, the ball must be kept on the ground, or else no higher off the ground than the height of the average player's knees.

3. Moreover, players may propel the ball only by reaching down and hitting it with their hands (clenched fists or otherwise). While in motion, the ball may bounce off a player, even off his or her foot while the player is running, but the player may not intentionally kick the ball or strike it with any part of the body except the hands.

4. Whenever the ball is kicked, or travels higher than a player's knees, or is held, it is placed on the grass where the foul occurred and put into play by the team opposing the team whose player committed the foul.

5. Whenever the ball leaves the court on a side, it is put into play at the point where it left the court by the team opposing the team whose player last touched the ball while it was still in play.

6. Teams may organize themselves in any way they desire to best protect their end of the court. Each team earns one point when its players get the ball over the opposing team's end of the court. The winning team is the first one to gain seven points.

"MOUNTED MEDIC" SNOWBALL WAR

Here's a new version of one of the oldest games in existence, the old fashioned snowball fight. Divide the group into two teams and play by the following rules:

1. Anyone hitting an opponent on the head is automatically out, even if it was done accidentally.

2. If you are hit by a snowball, you must fall to the ground and remain there until your "mounted medic" comes and "heals" you.

3. Each team is allowed one "mounted medic." This person must be a girl. Her "horse" must be a guy.

4. The "mounted medic" must stay on her horse at all times.

She may get off only when she must "heal" a soldier. She "heals" him by kissing him on the forehead. A girl is "healed" by being kissed by the medic's horse.

5. You may only be healed by your own "mounted medic."

6. Anyone hitting either a medic or her horse is automatically out, even if it was done accidentally.

7. Each team chooses one King.

8. The War is won by assassinating the opposing King, that is, by hitting him on the body, not limbs or head. If the King is hit on the limbs, he must fall to the ground and be healed by the "mounted medic."

9. Option: Kissing may be replaced by wrapping the "wounded" part with toilet paper.

MUDDY WATERS PILLOW FIGHT

This is a good game for camps. Individuals do battle seated on a ten inch diameter pole suspended a few feet over a creek or mudhole. You can dig the puddle if you don't own one. The object is to knock the competition off the pole and into the water with a pillow. This is a team action with points going to the winner's side. Teams should be comprised of about fifteen members. If the group is large enough a tournament may be played.

MUMMY

Select two or three guys to be "mummified." Each guy has two girls who wrap him up in toilet paper or paper towels from head to toe within a given time limit. The audience then judges to determine the best job.

NEEDLE IN THE HAYSTACK

In a big pile of hay, hide a bunch of large knitting needles, using different colored needles. Give the colors different values, either in points or in money, making the lighter (harder to find) colors more valuable. Turn the players loose, telling them to throw the hay up in the air for best results. They then bring the needles, as they find them, to the leader, who announces to the remainder of the group how many needles are left.

NOSE PENNY

The participants sit on chairs facing the audience. The player leans his head back. A penny is placed on his nose. The object is to wiggle the penny off his nose *without moving his head.* First to knock the penny off wins.

NOSE WASHING

Have three couples come to the front of the room. Place a glob of shaving cream on each boy's nose. From six feet away, the girls race to clean the soap off, by using squirt guns.

NO TRESPASSING

Tie a plastic-covered clothesline rope, approximately 20 feet long, to 2 folding chairs, so that the rope is about 8 inches off the floor. The rope should be in the center of the room. Also, be sure to make your rope with a masking tape flag approximately one foot from each chair. This is for the safety of whoever is "it."

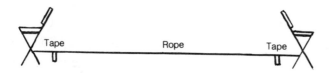

Choose one person to be "it" and divide the rest into two groups. Each group takes one end of the field (or room) facing the other group. Blindfold the "it" person and also give him some knee pads to protect his knees if the floor is hard or rough. The "it" person then takes his position, kneeling with one hand on the rope. He is free to move on his knees as long as he is touching the rope. On a signal each team hops on one foot across the rope to get to the other side. Team members must cross the rope without tripping or being tagged by the person who is "it." Before jumping over the rope, each person must announce his jump by clapping his hands together five times. Any "trespassers" (jumpers) caught become an obstacle for the next round. They lie face down parallel to the rope, leaving room on each side for the jumpers. The first person caught becomes the next "it."

NUT HUNT

Ahead of time, hide peanuts all over the room. Divide into teams and assign each team an animal name (Donkey, Cow, etc.). Each team also has a leader. The idea is to find all the peanuts. The team members hunt for them and as soon as a peanut is located, the person must get down on all fours and make his animal sound (Hee-Haw, etc.), until the team leader comes and collects the peanut. Then, the team member can go find more peanuts. The team leader with the most peanuts at the end of the time limit wins for his team.

NYLON GAME

Choose teams. Get all the old nylon stockings possible and put them in the middle of the room. Have everyone remove his shoes. One team sits in a circle around the pile. They are given one minute to put on all the nylons they can, one over the other, on one leg only. The team who gets the most nylons on wins.

NYLON RACE

Select two men and have them come to the front and be seated in chairs, facing the audience. Each is given a pair of nylon stockings and a pair of garden gloves. With the gloves on, they race to see who can put the nylons on in the fastest time. Shoes must be taken off, of course.

PAGE SCRAMBLE

Give each team a children's story book with titles such as "Waldo the Jumping Dragon," or "Big Albert Moves Into Town." The dumber the better. You must also make sure each book has the same number of pages. Before passing them out, however, carefully remove the pages from each book cover, and mix them up so that each team has a book with the correct number of pages . . . but not the correct pages. On a signal, the teams distribute the pages among team members and they

begin trading page for page with other team members. Thus
the area becomes a giant trading floor. The first team with a
completed book, with pages in the correct order, wins.

PEOPLE MACHINES

Divide up into groups of seven or eight. Each group has the
task of becoming a machine, such as washing machine, a tape
recorder, a record player, etc. Each individual must be a
working part with a suitable sound (electric cord with a hum, a
turntable with a soft whir, etc.). Each machine is then presented to the rest of the whole group for them to guess what is
being portrayed.

PICTURE PANIC

Divide group into two teams. Each team's captain is given a
pencil and pad. The director writes a word phrase on his pad
and shows it to the captains only. At the signal, they run to their
groups and draw a *picture* that gives their team a clue to the
word or phrase. First team to guess word or phrase wins.

PIE EATING CONTEST

It's old, but it's still one of the best fun things around. Have a
race in which guys (or girls) devour cream pies with no hands.
Put a time limit on, and give prizes for the most pie eaten, the
messiest face, the neatest eater, etc.

PILLOW BALANCE-BEAM BLAST

Take an old railroad tie or make your own narrow, raised
playing area. The two players stand at either end of the beam.
Each is given a pillow. At the signal, "go," each tries to knock
his opponent off the beam. The first one to touch the floor loses.
However, the winner must remain standing after the other
person falls.

PILLOW CASE RACE

In this relay, each participant races with both feet in a pillow
case. He must hop to a goal and back without stepping out of
the pillow case or ripping it.

PIN THE DONKEY ON THE TAIL

If you can get a live donkey (they are really not that hard to find), here is a variation of an old game. Hang a "tail," which can be a girl's fall or even a piece of old thick rope or something, on a fence, or a bale of hay, etc., and then put the donkey about 30 feet away. Have a group of about 6 guys try to get the donkey's rear end up against the tail for a time. The donkey hates to move in reverse, and usually will refuse to go anywhere, and provides a lot of laughs, but be careful that the guys are instructed to stay away from the donkey's hind feet.

PING-PONG BALL RACE

Select several players to race Ping-Pong balls. Each player gets a party blower (the type that uncoils when you blow it) and he pushes the ball across the floor using only his blower. He cannot blow directly on the ball or touch it in any way. First one across the finish line wins.

PING-PONG BASKETBALL

Have contestants bounce (at least one time, there is no limit otherwise) Ping-Pong balls into different size containers. Vary amount of points given depending upon difficulty (the smaller the container, the larger the amount of points given).

PING-PONG FLOUR BLOW

Have two fellows compete to see who can blow a Ping-Pong ball out of a round bowl in the fastest time. Each tries and is timed. Then, to make it even more difficult, they are to try it blindfolded. The first one does and is timed. Then the second one tries. But just before he blows, dump a cup of flour in the bowl.

PING-PONG PUFF

Players surround a sheet and pull it tight, under their chins so that is is flat. A Ping-Pong ball is placed in the center and players try to blow it to the other side. Each side of the sheet can be a team. Every time the ball hits someone, or goes over the edge, the team on that side gets a point. The team with the *least* amount of points wins. This may also be done with a table instead of a sheet, but the sheet is easier, and more fun.

POLISH BASEBALL

This is a great game for groups of 50 or more (25 per team). There are only 2 bases: home plate and first base (located approximately 120 feet from home). A regular baseball bat is used with a volley ball slightly mushy. There is no out of bounds. The ball may be hit in any direction. The pitcher is always from the team that is up. Each batter gets only one pitch. The batter does not have to accept the pitch but if he does swing, it counts as one pitch. Outs are made in the following manner:

1. A missed swing.
2. A fly ball that is caught.
3. A forced out at first base. (You cannot be forced out at home.)
4. Being touched by the ball. (A runner may be hit by a thrown ball or tagged out.)

Once a runner reaches the first base, he does not have to leave, until it is safe to do so. (Any amount of players may be on first base at the same time.) As soon as the team at bat has three outs, that team runs to the field and the fielding team immediately lines up and starts playing. They do not have to wait for the fielding team to get into position out in the field, or at home plate. You can have up to four games going at once on the same field but on different sides of the field, which can be very confusing, but a lot of fun. Each game needs a neutral umpire who judges "outs." The team with the most runs wins. Any amount of innings may be played.

POLISH FOOTBALL

Team 1 lines up in single file. The first line is the "kicker." The other team (Team 2) scatters around the field. As soon as the ball (kickball) is kicked, someone on Team 2 gets the ball and everyone lines up single file behind him. The ball is then passed over their heads (or between their legs) until it reaches the last person. Meanwhile the kicker on Team 1 runs around his teammates and they yell each lap. An out is made when the team in the field passes the ball the entire length of the team *before* the kicker makes one lap around his team.

POP BOTTLE PICKUP

Select several boys to see who can stand on one foot, with the other foot held up with his hand, and try to pick up a standing pop bottle with his teeth. Whoever can do it in the shortest time wins. If you fall over, you're out.

POTATO RACE

Teams line up and each player must push the potato along the floor to a goal and back using his nose only. No hands are allowed.

PULL OFF

This is a wild game which is easy to play and lots of fun. All the guys are to get inside a circle and huddle together in any position and lock arms. The girls attempt to pull the boys out of the circle any way they can. The guys try to stay in. The last guy to remain in the circle is the winner. Guys cannot fight the girls . . . all they are allowed to do is to hang on and try to stay in.

RIDE THE TUB

For this game, you will need to get an old washtub big enough to stand in. Through the two handles of the tub (over the top) a six-foot long pole or pipe is placed. The two ends of the pole are then placed on the seats of two chairs so that the tub hangs suspended between the two chairs. Next, hang four hats on the backs of the chairs, two on each chair. Select three players. One at a time, they are to stand in the tub with one leg on each side of the pole, and with a broom, knock the hats off the chair. They must balance themselves in the tub without holding on to anything and knock the hats down before they fall out of the tub, which inevitably happens. The one who gets the most hats off is the winner.

RING ON A STRING

Have a group sit in a circle on chairs. Take a piece of string and have every person hold the string with both hands (except for one person who stands in the middle). Tie the string at both ends so it is one big circle with a ring (the larger the better) on the string that can slide all the way around. Have the members of the group slide their hands along the string and pass the ring along as they try to hide it from the person in the middle. He tries to guess who has the ring by going around the circle (from the inside) and tapping different people's hands. When a person's hand is tapped he opens his hands to reveal whether he or she has the ring. When the person in the middle taps someone with the ring they switch places. This may be used with small groups of 8 to 20 people.

ROLLING PIN THROW

This is a hilarious idea for family and church picnics, adult recreation or youth. Have a contest to see which women can throw a wooden rolling pin the longest distance. Results are side-splitting!

ROUNDUP

All the players are divided into two teams with the same number of boys and girls on each team. The girls of each team are the cowboys and the boys the cows. The cows must stay on their hands and knees throughout the game. The object of the game is this: the girls of each team try to get the cows of the opposing team into an area designated as the corral. The girls can drag, carry, etc., a cow to that area. Of course, the cows can resist but must stay on hands and knees. After a designated time interval, the team with the most cows in their corral wins.

RUN THE GAUNTLET

This old game is one of the best outdoor co-ed games available. Girls are given rolled-up newspapers, and they are lined up in two single file lines. The two lines are parallel, facing each other with approximately three to four feet between them. The boys tie balloons to their seats (on their pant belt loops) and must "run the gauntlet," that is, they must run between the two lines of girls who try to pop the balloons by hitting them with the newspapers. The object is to see which boy(s) can avoid having their balloon popped.

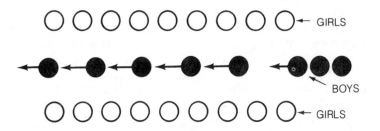

SACK RACE

This is an old game that is always successful with nearly every age group. Obtain a number of burlap bags (potato sacks) and divide the group into teams. The teams line up, and the first player in each line gets into the sack, feet first, and holds the sack up while hopping around a goal and back. On completion, the next player gets the sack, does the same thing, and the first team to finish is the winner.

SEA FOOD SPECIAL

A number of events may be developed by using frogs, crabs, turtles, snails. Of course, the traditional frog-jumping contest is always a winner, but many other ideas may be adapted. Turtle races, crab races, turtle football (first one to cross opposing team's "goal line"). What makes these events appealing is publicity and elaborateness. Each contestant (or team) should have a week to choose and train his entry. Each entry should be elaborately decorated or painted. The "judge" should dress accordingly with loud horns, whistles, and guns to start and finish the race. These events are natural for radio and television publicity.

SHOE SCRAMBLE

Everyone removes his shoes and places them into one big pile. Divide the girls into two teams, and then they must run to the pile of shoes and locate one pair of boy's shoes. (Try to make sure that there are the same number of boys playing this game as girls.) Each girl must then find the owner of the pair of shoes she picked off the pile. That boy then becomes the girl's partner and he must then go to the pile and find her shoes from her description of them. The first team to get their shoes on wins.

SHOE SHUCKING RACE

Divide into groups of six (girls must wear pants to play). Each team member must lie on his back with his feet in the air, feet meeting in the center of the circle. A container of water (dishpan) is placed on the elevated feet. The object is for each member to remove his shoes without spilling his water. The team to win is the one with the most shoes off at the three-minute time limit.

SHOE STRETCH

Get two old pairs of men's shoes. Take out the shoestrings, punch a hole in the back of the shoes, and tie a four-foot piece of elastic to each shoe. Place two chairs about twenty feet apart and tie the other ends of the elastic to the legs of the chairs (one pair of shoes on each chair). Now get two boy volunteers to play the game. The boys each put on a pair of the shoes (they are not tied, but loose on their feet). The boys are to walk to each other, stretching the elastic, and exchange shoes without using their hands. Have people sitting in the two chairs to weight them. If the shoes snap back to the chair, the player must start over from there. Have several two-men teams compete to see which can do it in the fastest time.

SHOE TIE

Select three couples to play this game. The boys should be wearing shoes that have shoestrings (not boots, etc.). The boys are seated and one of their shoes is untied. The girls must re-tie the shoe using one hand and anything else (except the other hand). The girl to finish first wins.

SILLY SOCCER

Divide your group into two teams. In a large open field, place two pylons 100 to 150 feet apart. The object is to hit the opposing team's pylon with the ball. There are no boundaries, and the pylon may be hit from any direction. All other soccer rules apply. For added confusion with a large group, throw in a second ball.

SINGING CHARADES

Divide your group into smaller groups. Each group sends one person to the center of the room where he and other entries are given the name of a song (the leader whispers). Each rushes back to his own team with paper and pencil and draws out a picture which he thinks best describes the song. (No words may be written or said by the artist.) The team tries to guess what the song is and when they get it immediately sing it out. The first team to sing the correct song wins. Each team sends another entry. The game may be repeated for each team member or until the leader wishes to stop. This is a great game for informal Christmas parties, when you use carols for songs.

SLIDE STORIES

Divide the group into teams of five to ten each. Provide each team with twenty or more slides of various things: people, objects, travel, nature, whatever you can throw in. Each team must make up a story using as many of the slides as possible. Set a time limit and have each team project its "slide story" for the rest of the group. The most creative, funniest, longest, etc. wins.

SNOWFIGHT

Two teams are separated by a row of chairs and given a six-foot stack of newspaper. They are then given one minute to wad up the paper. When the signal is given, each team then attempts to throw the most paper on the other team's side by the time limit. Each round (usually about 4 rounds per night) is separated by a 30-second break to find everyone who might be buried in the mountain of paper. Team with most paper on their side loses; however, there is always such a mess that a tie is declared. *Caution:* The only way to stop the throwing between rounds is to give the last person who throws something a good penalty (pie in the face, etc.).

SOUND-OFF

Here's a fun game that requires some audio-visual equipment. Obtain two home movie projectors, two cassette recorders, and either two different cartoons (that can be shown on the home movie projectors) or two copies of the same cartoon. Divide the crowd into teams.

First, show the two cartoons (or comedies) to both teams. They should be silent films with titles written on the screen. Then give each team one of the projectors, one of the films, and one of the cassette recorders (with a blank tape) and have them record a "soundtrack" for their film. If the same cartoon is used for both teams, then a contest may be called to see which team can do the best job. Any sound effects, music, or dialogue may be used. Allow plenty of time for the team's creative efforts.

SPOOL PONG

Place two spools, one on each side of the net on the center line of the table about eighteen inches from the ends of the table. Place an extra Ping-Pong ball on top of each. Add five points to your score if you can knock your opponent's ball off the spool. Score the game normally otherwise.

SQUEEZE PLAY

Two people face each other. Place a large balloon between them. Time the pair to see how fast they can break the balloon by body pressure alone. The fastest pair wins. The slowest gets a penalty.

SQUIRM RACE

Place a volleyball (or ball of similar size) between the foreheads of a boy and a girl couple. Without using their hands, they must work the ball down to their knees and back up again. Their hands must be kept behind their backs and the two must start over if they drop the ball. Couples do not have to be of the opposite sex. Two guys or two girls will work fine but a boy-girl couple usually adds to the fun of this event.

STEAL THE BACON IN THE ROUND

Draw a large circle with lines for line-up which are separate from the circle. Locate the center. (Circle diameter, approximately 15 feet. Lime works well in field or paint on black top.) By curving the lineup line, all the kids can see the activity without interfering with the action of the game.

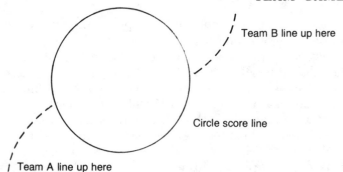

Team B line up here

Circle score line

Team A line up here

Place the "bacon" (an old shirt, a sponge, or small ball) in the center. The players line up. The first person on each team, on the blowing of a whistle, runs to the center and takes the bacon over the circle score line. If the person possessing the bacon is tagged, then the tagging person receives the point. If, after a pre-determined time (say, 30 seconds) no one picks up the bacon, blow the whistle and the next two players may join the two in the circle. When two team members are working together, they may pass the bacon between themselves.

Advantages:

1. The circle allows for a person to run in any direction to score.
2. The teams do not have to be equal; in fact, it is better if they are not equal, so that the players never compete against the same person on future turns.
3. You do not have to number off players or call out numbers.
4. The game handles large numbers of players and all get a turn.

STILTS STEAL THE BACON

This works best with four teams. Have the teams line up forming a square (each team on one side of the square). The teams need to be numbered from one to however many are on each team (equal number on each). A pair of stilts is given to each team and placed about six feet away, centered and in front of each team. When the leader calls a number, those with that number from each team run to the stilts, mount them and try to go after the "bacon" on stilts and also try to get the bacon back across their side. A volleyball will make the best "bacon" and should be placed in the middle. The team with the highest score wins.

STRUNG OUT

Have any number of teams stand in straight lines. Each team gets a cold spoon with a 20' piece of string tied to it. The spoon should be just out of the freezer. The object is to see how many people you can lace together by taking the spoon and passing it through your clothing. (Neck down to ankle). The first contestant holds end of string in mouth. This is *not* timed. Anything goes, from bending, lying down, crouching, etc. Anything to get more string out.

TAIL-GRAB

Divide the group into any number of equal "chains" (a line of people in which each person grips the wrist of the one in front of him). The last person in the chain has a handkerchief "tail" dangling behind. The object is for each front person to snatch the tail from another line. The fun is trying to maneuver to get someone else's tail while trying to keep your own.

THE TEAM DIVISION GAME

The following is a good game and may be used as a method for randomly assigning kids to a team for further team competition or discussion groups. Here is how it works:

Each team is assigned a two-color combination (use construction paper), distinct from any other (for team identification). The same color may be used twice but each time with a different second color. For each color combination (hence, each team to play), place two sheets of paper on each other and cut out two circles of equal size, using the entire sheet. Then cut each set of circles into any number of randomshaped pieces. Each set of circles cut into three pieces yields 6 pieces of each color (12 pieces).

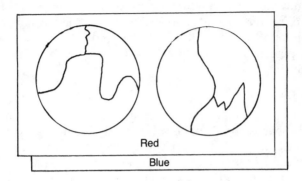

Then discard half of the 12 pieces so that you are left with 2 circles composed of pieces of the two basic colors.

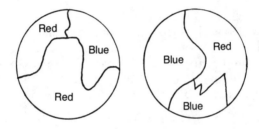

Note that you are left with 6 pieces which match into circles but not necessarily of the same color. This allows up to 6 members per team. For 7 or 8 per team, cut circles into 4 pieces each; for any number less than 6, simply discard some from above diagram leaving one circle only partially complete. Paper clip the combinations together in a stack so that at the last minute, you can discard enough to result in the exact amount to be on each team. Repeat this process for *each* team's color combination and place them in a paper bag for drawing.

To begin with, everyone draws one piece out of the paper bag. They must then match their piece to the others who have the matching portions to their circle. Explain that:

1. Colors do not necessarily match.

2. Once you match with someone, stick together.

3. Do not exchange pieces with anyone.

4. After all are matched (this will take some time, but help out if it takes more than 15 minutes), there will be many groups of 3 standing around together (or 2 or 4, in some cases, if that's how you set it up). Then combine all the groups with the color combinations chosen for each team into that team, e.g., all those with circles of red and blue (will be two groups) gather together and become Team A and so on.

You may make signs for each team, using color combinations that may be hung on the wall, or that the kids may wear around their necks, or whatever.

TEN TOES ON THE ROCKS

Fill two pans with crushed ice and place ten marbles in the bottom of the pans, underneath the ice. Two boys must remove their shoes and socks and try to get the marbles out of the pan using only their toes. They may not turn the pan over, or spill any ice. The first to get all the marbles out of the pan is the winner.

THREAD THE NEEDLE

For this game you will need two table knives (the old fashioned kind that had a "neck" between the blade and the handle), and two balls of string (medium weight).

Divide the group into two teams. The teams start at exactly the same time to . . . "thread the "needle" (the knife with the end of the string tied tightly to the neck of the knife) down through their shirt and one pants leg (or . . . their blouse and skirt or shorts etc.). This person then passes the "needle" on to the person behind him to do the same and on down to the end of the line. Each team member is constantly busy, for he is continually feeding "thread" (the string) along the way, so that there is enough thread to connect the entire team.

When the last person has "threaded the needle," he then begins the process of "unthreading the needle"! This is done by pulling up on the string and getting the "needle" (knife) up, through, and out of his slacks and shirt (or whatever!). This takes constant team work, for when "unthreading the needle," each team member works to pass the slack in the string along so at the end, the first person in line has the string in a neat ball again. And the team has been able to complete the whole procedure without the "thread" becoming detached from the "needle" at any given time!

The fun part of the game is to try in every way to make it a speedy relay. The fun mounts as members help teammates along yet keeping the "thread" from getting knotted, the "needle" from getting stuck, etc.

This game has proven to be an excellent, exciting game for Junior high through older adults.

THREE-LEGGED JEANS RACE

Prior to the meeting, sew several pairs of old jeans together in the following manner. Rip out the outside seam of alternate legs on alternate pairs of jeans and sew the two pairs together. Use baggy jeans. Couples must get into the jeans, and at a signal, race to the goal.

THREE-LEGGED RACE

Two players from each group compete for this event. They stand side by side and the two legs nearest each other are tied together. On the signal to go, they race to the goal and back.

THREE-LEGGED SOCCER

Couples are tied just as in three-legged race (including goalies), then teamed for soccer. One group did it in the fall on a large tomato field with plenty of overripe tomatoes all over the playing area. Make sure players are instructed to wear long pants.

TINY TIM RACE

Divide the group into teams. On a signal, each team must line up according to height, with the shortest person on one end and the tallest on the other. The last team to do so, or any team that is out of the proper order, is the loser.

TIRE BOWLING (WITH PEOPLE PINS)

Just about any service station or tire store will gladly give you some old tire casings (get a variety of sizes and let the players "choose" their own). Use either 12 or 20 players total per setup. Divide the group and while one half bowls the other acts as the pins. Bowlers should be a set distance from the "pins," say 30-40 feet. The people pins should be set up just like regular 10 pins (or 6) spaced about 2-3 feet from each other. The pins are allowed to try and avoid the tire as it comes at them *but* they must keep both feet together unmoved. If they move either foot at all, the bowler gets the pin. It is best to mark the spot where the pins should stand with a small object like a rock. Let half the team bowl each time, then switch places. Next time up, let the other half have their turn. Scoring may be either straight number of people hit or strikes (3 touched with first roll) and spares (3 touched with two rolls). If the last is used, have each pin hit equal 3 pins, so if 2 are hit it gives a score of 6. The trick to hitting as many as possible is to roll the tire wobbly and try to get it to fall down in the midst of the pins, striking several as it falls. Caution: These casings are dirty, so wear grubbies and have washing facilities handy.

TIRE GRAN PRIX

Lay out a course around the church buildings or down roads that are closed to traffic, and give everyone an old tire. Then have a race rolling the tires around the course. For larger groups, make it a team relay, with players stationed every 50 yards along the course. The tire is passed on at each "pit stop" to a fresh "driver." The first player (or team) to complete the course wins.

For added fun, allow players to kick, knock over, or in any way impede the progress of the opposing racers. Old tires may be borrowed from a cooperative tire dealer or service station.

TOILET PAPER RACE

Guys (or girls) race to see who can unroll a roll of toilet paper by pushing it along the ground with their *noses*. The first person to unroll the entire roll, or cross the finish line wins. For

a switch, have other contestants do it in reverse, that is, roll it
back up in the fastest time.

TUG OF WAR

An old-fashioned tug of war never fails to be a winner. Just
get a good thick, long rope and put one team on each end of it.
Whichever team can pull the other one across the line or into a
nice big mudhole in the middle is the winner. For laughs, put
grease all over the rope and see what happens. . . .

TUG-O-WAR IN THE ROUND

Get a large rope about 24 feet in length and tie (or splice) the
two ends together, making one round rope. Four teams line up
on four sides of a square. In the center of the square, the rope is
placed opened out into a circle. The teams should be equal in
size and each team should number off from one on up. The
leader then calls out a number and the four players (one from
each team) with that number grab one side of the rope and try
to get back across their team's line. As soon as a player crosses
the line (pulling the rope), he is declared the winner. Continue
until everyone has had a try.

TURKEY

This may be done at Thanksgiving. In commemoration of the
holiday, you may have a little *competition* to see which group
can do the best job of "decorating a turkey." Divide into three
or four groups. Give each a paper sack full of goodies . . . an old
pair of nylons, a roll of toilet paper, scissors, scotch tape, crepe
or tissue paper, newspaper or anything else you might be able
to think of that will contribute to making a person look like a
turkey. Set a time limit. You explain to the players what they
are to do, then divide the groups. Have the group select one
person to be the "turkey." Give them three or four minutes to
do the decorating and then have the whole group be judges and
decide the winner by applause.

WADDLE TO THE BOTTLE

In this relay, teams race with players carrying a small coin
(penny, dime) between their knees. They must successfully

drop the coin into a milk bottle or jar placed 15 or 20 feet away without using their hands. If the coin is dropped along the way, the player must start over.

WATER BALLOON BLITZ

Divide into two teams. Give each team 15 minutes to fill balloons (make sure there are plenty of water outlets). When the starting signal is given, everyone unloads balloons until stock is finished. Winner is the driest team. Be sure to announce beforehand that any participant may wear any protective items he wants (garbage can tops, goggles, etc.). Suggested number of water balloons to give out:

One team of 50 .... 200 balloons
One team of 100 .... 400 balloons
One team of 150 .... 600 balloons
One team of 200 .... 800 balloons

WATER BALLOON CATAPULT

This has to be one of the most exciting and fun game ideas you'll ever use. Tie a long piece of surgical tubing to two stakes. Punch two holes in a half football and slide on to the center of the tubing. Place water balloons in half football, pull back, and let her fly. You should be able to lob balloons up to forty yards without any trouble. Of course, you can have two teams face each other in battle or try to lob the balloons directly at certain targets. *Caution:* This may be dangerous and destructive. If balloons are lobbed low or at close range, they can dent a car, break windows and people's heads.

WATER BALLOON SHOT PUT

This is a simple game to see who can toss a water balloon "shot put" style the farthest. To give the players added incentive, the leader may stand at a place just out of reach of the shot-putters, and they use him as a target.

WATER BALLOON TOSS

Couples line up facing each other, and are given a water balloon which they toss back and forth at a signal of some sort. Each time they move one step farther apart. Last couple to keep their water balloon intact are the winners.

WATER BALLOON VOLLEYBALL

Water Balloon Volleyball is played similarly to conventional volleyball. But this is more fun. Set up your volleyball net as usual, and divide the people into equal sides. This type of volleyball is not restricted to the conventional 6-member, 9-member team, but any number may play. Of course, the main difference in this game is that instead of using a regular volleyball, you use a water balloon for the ball. The service takes place from the back line and each team is allowed three tosses and three catches to get the water balloon over the net to the opposing team. The opposing team then has three tosses and three catches to get the ball back across the net. The balloon is continually tossed back and forth across the net until, finally, breakage occurs. When the balloon breaks, the side on which it breaks does not score, but rather, the opposite team gets the point, without regard to who did the serving. Spikes are allowed, but again, if the balloon breaks on the team who is doing the spiking, the other team is awarded the point. The team that then wins the point, regardless of which team it is, is the team that continues to serve until service is broken. The game is played to a regular volleyball score of 15, at which time sides of the net are changed and the game resumes. All other rules in regular volleyball are in effect for this game, such as out-of-bound lines, not being able to cross over the net with your hand, or falling into the net with your body.

Another variation of this game which proves to be even more fun, is to include 30 or 40 members of each team and insert into play 4 or 5 water balloons; so that there are several opportunities for returns, spikes, and services all at the same time. The rules for this game are the same as for the one-ball system. There is no official scoring for this game. The winning team is simply the driest team at the end of an allotted period of time.

WATER BALLOON WHOMPIES

This game is a great way to cool off on a hot day. No one wins, it's just fun to do. Team members each get three to five water balloons. Draw a circle on the ground and the entire team sits down inside the circle, while another team lobs water balloons at them. The sitting team cannot move. The throwing team must stay behind a given line, throw the balloons under-handed, and on a ten-foot arc. Any one breaking the rules must sit down on a full water balloon. The teams trade places when one team runs out of balloons. Give a prize to the driest team.

WATER-BUCKET RACE

Use either a gallon paint can, a half-gallon milk carton, or a gallon plastic milk carton. Put this object, empty, on a wire or thin rope tied at both ends to something solid. Do this over an open space. Then choose up two teams. Give each one a water hose with water running through it. The object is to see who can push the container to the opponent's end first. The water from the hoses just happens to come falling down on everyone involved.

WILLIAM TELL

Make "Candle Hats" by either putting candles on top of real hats, or by putting candles on the bottom of saucers, then tying the saucers on a person's head with ribbon. Use your own creativity here. The important thing is to get candles on top of a person's head.

Next, give the players squirt guns, and with the candles lit on their heads, they try to put out the other's candle by squirting it out. They cannot move their feet. The idea is simply to keep your candle lit and put out your opponent's.

A variation of this would be to use couples. The guys wear the candles on their heads and the girls get the squirt guns. Each couple stands about ten feet apart. On a signal, the girls try to put out the candle on the boys head with the squirt gun. The first to do so wins.

WINDBAG HOCKEY

A great way to play "hockey" in a small, confined area is to get teams down on all fours, and place Ping-Pong ball in the center. The teams must then blow the Ping-Pong ball through their goals (a doorway or the legs of a chair, etc.). without touching the ball. If the ball touches a player, he goes to the "penalty box" and no "goalies" are used. Two balls at once can make the game even more exciting.

RELAYS

Relays

APPLE CIDER RELAY

Divide into teams and give each team member a straw. The object is to see which team can consume a gallon of apple cider first. You control the contest with a whistle. Each time you blow the whistle, the kids run to the jugs and drink as much cider as possible, using the straw (one player from each team at a time). Make sure that teams stay in line so that everyone has a turn. Also make sure that your group smart aleck doesn't lift the jug and swig half of it while you're scratching your ear. For hilarious results, give the players who like apple cider a short time to drink and give the ones who can't stand it a long turn.

ARMPIT AND EGG RELAY

Half the team lines up on each side of the room. First person races to the other side with a spoon in his mouth and an egg on it. The teammate on the other side takes the egg and puts it in his armpit and runs back across the room. He must drop the egg from his armpit onto the next person's spoon.

BACK-UP RELAY

Have two people race to a point, face each other and hold their arms straight up in the air. Someone from their team places a ball between them. They must simultaneously make a 360 degree turn without the ball falling to the ground. They return to their team and the next two people do the same. If the ball falls, they must start over.

BALLOON BROOM RELAY

This is a team relay game — good for indoor parties and events. Each team gets a broom and a round balloon. On "go" the players "sweep" the balloon to a point across the room, and then *carry* the balloon back on the end of the broom (or bat it through the air with the broom). First team to have all its players make the trip wins.

BALLOON POP RELAY

Divide your group into teams. The teams line up single file at a starting line. A chair is placed about 30 feet away. Each team member has a deflated balloon. One at a time, kids run to the chair, blow up the balloon, tie it, pop it by sitting on it, and go to the end of the team line. First team to pop all of its balloons wins.

BAT-ROUND RELAY

Divide your group into teams. Each team gets a baseball bat which is placed on one end of the playing area, with the team lined up at the other end. The object of this relay is for each team member to run to the bat, put his forehead on the bat (in a vertical position) and run around the bat ten times while in that position. He then returns to the team, usually so dizzy that getting back to the team is a difficult and fun-to-watch experience.

"BETCHA CAN'T REMEMBER EVERYTHING TO DO" RELAY

Teams line up in a single file line about 15 feet from a basketball goal (they would be standing at the foul line). At the signal, the first two people leap frog to a designated spot where the first one in line then continues on by rolling a peanut with his nose to another designated spot (the second player goes back to the front of the line). After rolling the peanut with his nose, he then takes a spoon and puts a Ping-Pong ball in it and walks to another designated spot. Then he takes a basketball and goes to the back of the line. His team members (standing in a straight line) spread their legs apart and the player then sends the ball between their legs and runs to the front of the line to catch up with the rolling basketball. When he successfully catches it, he must then make a basket. After making a basket, he then takes a small glass of coke, drinks it, and burps. When this whole routine is finished, the next one in line goes through the whole thing. (leap frog, peanut roll, Ping-Pong ball in a spoon, etc.). The winning team is the one that has every member participate fully in each event and finishes first.

BLANKET RIDE RELAY

One girl is chosen to ride the blanket throughout the race (a substitute may stand by in case of injury or dizziness). Other team members (preferably boys) line up behind the end line. The girl is positioned on the blanket (sitting crosslegged) holding on tightly, and the first boy in line grabs the blanket and assumes a pulling position. On signal, the boy begins running while pulling the blanket all the way around the room and around a marker at the far end, then back to the starting point where the next boy in line takes over. The blanket must be pulled completely over the line before the next boy may take hold. The first team to complete all rounds wins.

BOTTLE FILL RELAY

Each team appoints one boy to lie down face up with head toward starting line and holding an empty Coke bottle on his head. Each team member fills a cup (made of nonbendable material) with water, runs to bottle and pours in water until it is gone. He then runs back and as soon as he crosses the starting line the next contestant runs out with a cup of water and does the same.

BOY RELAY

Boys line up in several teams. Girl members of their teams divide in half and each half lines up on one side of their boys' team. So you have a line of boys with a short line of girls on each side of them. At a signal, four girls from each line — two from each side of the boys — pick up the first boy. One girl takes one leg, another the other leg and one girl takes each arm. They then carry the boy across the room and deposit him on a chair. Then the girls race back to the team, get to the end of the line and the next four carry the next boy. The first team to carry all boys across is the winner. Girls will have to carry more than one boy.

BROOM JUMP RELAY

Divide into teams. Team members should stand two abreast. First couple of each team is given a broom. At signal "go" the couple must each grab one end of the broom and run back through their team (broom is held just above floor). Everyone in the line must jump over the broom back to the front of the line. Broom is carried by hands only — no throwing. Then second couple repeats, etc. Game is won by first team with original couple again heading the team.

BROOM TWIST RELAY

Teams line up in normal relay race fashion. At a point some 20 or 30 feet away, a team captain or leader stands and holds a broom. When the game begins, each player runs to his team leader, takes the broom, holds it against his or her chest with the broom end (the bristles) up in the air over his head. Then, looking up at the broom, the player must turn around as fast as possible ten times, while the leader counts the number of turns. Then the player hands the broom back to the leader, runs back to the team, and tags the next player who does the same. Players become very dizzy and the results are hilarious.

BUMPER BOX RELAY

For this relay, you need to obtain a large refrigerator box for each team. Each player then gets inside the box, standing up, with the box over his head and the open end of the box down to the floor. On a signal, the players then race to the opposite wall or goal and back while receiving directions from their teammates who must yell them out from behind the starting line. Since the players cannot see, they run into each other, go the wrong way, and the results are really funny. For an added dimension to this game, decorate the boxes with wild colors, team names, or whatever.

CATERPILLAR RELAY

This is a great game for camps. Have the kids bring their sleeping bags to the meeting, and have races in them, head first. Simply line the teams up, relay style, and the first person in line gets in the sleeping bag, head first, and races to a certain point and back. Of course, he cannot see where he is going, so the team has to shout out directions to him. Each person on the team must do this, and the first team finished is the winner. If you prefer, you may have the kids crawl in their sleeping bags (like a caterpillar) which is slower, but safer.

CHARIOT RACE RELAY

Each team chooses sets of two boys and one girl. The number of these sets depends on the size of the teams involved. The two boys face each other and lock their arms, right with right, and left with left. That way the boys' arms are criss-crossed. The girl sits up on the boys' arms, and the boys then race around a goal and back. The next set of players get ready and leave as soon as the previous set returns.

CLOTHESPIN RELAY

String a clothesline from one end of the room to the other, shoulder high to the average person. Place clothespins on the line. Teams line up facing the line. The object is to run to the line, remove one clothespin with your teeth (no hands), and bring it back to the team. All team members do the same in relay fashion.

DOUBLE DUTY WATER RELAY

For this relay each team needs: a wastebasket size container that will hold water reasonably well, a #10 tin can, a pop bottle, and a large supply of water (such as a barrel continuously replenished by a hose). Anything that each team can fill their cans from without interferring with the other team(s) will do. This relay should take place outdoors. Place a sturdy chair for each team about fifty feet away from the starting line, facing the line. Place each wastebasket on the line, its team lined up nearby, boy-girl, boy-girl. Front boy has the can filled with water, front girl has the empty pop bottle. At the starting signal they run to the chair, girl sits on the chair and holds the bottle upright on her head for her teammate to fill, using the *unbent* can. Girls should not wear good clothes. When the bottle is full or the can is empty, whichever comes first, they run to the line and she empties the bottle into the wastebasket, while he refills the can and gives it to the next guy. This pair takes its turn and so on to the end of the team. If the wastebasket isn't full yet, have the boys and girls reverse roles. First team to fill its basket wins. Works best with two large teams.

EGG AND SPOON RELAY

Each player on the team gets a spoon. The teams line up and a dozen eggs are placed on one end of the line. The players must then pass the eggs down the line using the spoons only. You are not allowed to touch the eggs with your hands, except for the first player who puts the egg on his spoon and starts it down the line. The winning team is the one who gets the most eggs down the line (unbroken) in the fastest time.

ELASTIC BAND RELAY

In preparation for this game, cut a strip of inch-wide elastic 36 inches long. Overlap one inch and stitch on a sewing machine. The result will be a large elastic circle.

Break group into teams of eight to twelve players. Supply each team with an elastic band. At the starting signal, the first player brings the band over his head and body before passing it on to the next player on the team. The first team to have all the players pass the elastic band over their bodies is the winning team.

Variations may have the players passing the elastic band up from the feet, or couples passing the band over both bodies at once.

FILL THE BOTTLE RELAY

One fellow puts a coke bottle in his back pocket (if it will fit).

Girls (or the rest of the team) line up and get dixie cups. The guy stands at one end of the line and a pail of water is at the other end. The idea is to transport the water, passing it from cup to cup, from the pail to the coke bottle. First group to do so wins. The guy's pants usually get soaked.

FILL THE MAT RELAY

Each team is given two mattresses on which to perform. A description is called out and on whistle, each team then begins to fulfill the description. First team to accurately fulfill description is the winner. Suggested descriptions: 1. 14 players standing shoulder to shoulder, facing in alternate directions. 2. 15 players in one huge pyramid (pyramid must remain standing). 3. 10 contestants lying in a circle with feet together and holding hands — looks like a huge wheel. 4. 4 people standing on their heads — one in each corner of the mattress. 5. 5 pyramids of 3 people each. 6. 6 girls and 2 boys each doing a back bend. 7. 12 players lying side by side with heads and feet in alternate directions. 8. 3 piles of 5 players each — must be lying on top of one another's backs. 9. 2 piles of 10 players high — each sitting on one another's backs. 9. 2 piles of 10 players high — each sitting on one another's laps.

FLOUR AND PRUNE RELAY

Fill two large roaster-type pans with flour. The pans are placed 20 yards apart. Place prunes in each pan (the number of which is equal to the number on a team). Each team number must retrieve one prune using only his mouth and return to the starting line.

FOOTBALL RELAY

This is a good relay race for couples. Each couple must race to a goal and back with a football wedged between them, chin to chin, back to back, and lastly side to side. In other words, each couple races three times. If the ball is dropped, the couple must start over on that particular lap.

FOREHEAD RACE

This relay is for couples on a team. Each couple races to a

point and back carrying a grapefruit or balloon between their foreheads. If it is dropped, they must start over.

GRAPEFRUIT PASS

This is a good co-ed relay game. Teams line up boy-girl, boy-girl, etc. A grapefruit is started at one end of the line and must be passed down the line under the chins of the players. No hands are allowed. If the grapefruit is dropped, it must be started at the front of the line again.

HAND-IN-GLOVE RELAY

This is a relay game in which the teams stand in line and pass a pair of gloves from one end to the other. The first person puts the gloves on, then the next person takes them off and puts them on himself. Each person takes the gloves off the person in front of him and puts them on himself. All fingers of the hand must fit in the fingers of the gloves. Options: Use rubber kitchen gloves or large work gloves.

HAPPY HANDFUL RELAY

This relay may be easily adapted for indoor or outdoor use. Assemble two identical sets of at least 12 miscellaneous items (i.e., 2 brooms, 2 balls, 2 skillets, 2 rolls of bathroom tissue, 2 ladders, etc.). Use your imagination to collect an interesting variety of identical pairs of objects. Place the two sets of objects on two separate tables.

Line up a team for each table. The first player for each team runs to his table, picks up one item of his choice, runs back to his team and passes the item to the second player. The second player carries the first item back to the table, picks up another item and carries both items back to the third player. Each succeeding player carries the items collected by his teammates to the table, picks up one new item and carries them all back to the next player. The game will begin rapidly, but the pace will slow as each player decides which item to add to a growing armload of items. It will also take increasingly longer for one player to pass his burden to the next player in line.

Once picked up, an item may not touch the table or floor. Any item which is dropped in transit or transfer must be returned to the table by the leader. No one may assist the giving and receiving players in the exchange of items except through coaching. The first team to empty its table wins.

HOUNDS AND HARES

This is a good camp game best played where there is a lot of space. Best time to play is at night. Two teams are chosen. One team (the Hares) is given 100 sheets of newspaper. They leave base 5 minutes before the second team (the Hounds) give chase. The Hares affix a sheet of newspaper at eye level approximately every 100 feet. The Hares must use all their newspaper and then get back to base before the Hounds can overtake them. If they safely make it back to base, they win.

INNER TUBE RELAY

Each team chooses ten couples (or as many as you have). The couples should be of the same sex, rather than boy-girl couples. Each team then lines up in different corners of the room, if that arrangement is possible. Inner tubes (one for each team) are placed in the center of the room. Each couple must run to the inner tube, and squeeze through the tube together, starting with the tube over their heads and working it down. The first team to have all ten couples complete the stunt are the winners.

LEMON PASS

In this relay, teams pass a lemon down the line using only their bare feet. The lemon is held between both feet cupped in the arches of the feet, and the players must lie on their backs. The first team to get the lemon passed all the way down the line wins.

LIFESAVER RELAY

Divide the group into two lines and give each player a toothpick which he will place in his mouth. The leader will place a lifesaver on the toothpick of the players at the head of each line. It is then passed from toothpick to toothpick until it reaches the end of the line. If it is dropped before it reaches the end of the line, it must be started all over again at the beginning of the line. The winning team is the one whose lifesaver reaches the end of the line first.

MIXED-UP RELAY

This is a different kind of relay race in which each contestant does something different. What the contestants do is determined by the directions in a bag at the other end of the relay course.

At the beginning of the race, each team is lined up single file as usual. On a signal, the first person on each team runs to the other end of the course to a chair. On the chair is a bag containing instructions written on separate pieces of paper. The contestant draws one of the instructions, reads it, and follows it as quickly as possible. Before returning to the team, the contestant must tag the chair. The contestant then runs back and tags the next runner. The relay proceeds in this manner and the team that uses all of its instructions first is the winner. Below are a few examples of directions:

1. Run around the chair 5 times while continuously yelling, "The British are coming, the British are coming."

2. Run to the nearest person on another team and scratch his head.

3. Run to the nearest adult in the room and whisper, "You're no spring chicken."

4. Stand on one foot while holding the other in your hand, tilt your head back, and count, "10, 9, 8, 7, 6, 5, 4, 3, 2, 1, Blast Off!"

5. Take your shoes off, put them on the wrong foot, and then tag your nearest opponent.

6. Sit on the floor, cross your legs, and sing the following: "Mary had a little lamb, little lamb, little lamb, Mary had a little lamb, its fleece was white as snow."

7. Go to the last person on your team and make 3 different "funny-face" expressions, then return to the chair before tagging your next runner.

8. Put your hands over your eyes and snort like a pig 5 times and meow like a cat 5 times.

9. Sit in the chair, fold your arms, and laugh hard and loud for 5 seconds.

10. Run around the chair backwards 5 times while clapping your hands.

11. Go to a blond-headed person and keep asking, "Do blonds really have more fun?", until they answer.

12. Run to someone not on your team and kiss his or her hand and gently pinch his or her cheek.

MESSAGE RELAY

The following is a good team game. Teams divide in half and stand a distance away. Type out a crazy message on a piece of paper (one for each team) and give it to the first member who opens it, reads it, wads it up and throws it on the ground. He *runs* to the next person on his team at the other side and whispers it in his ear. Then he runs back and tells it to the next person and so on until the last person runs to the supervisor and whispers it to him. The team closest to the original message wins. Accuracy, not time, is most important, but they must run. Sample message. "Mrs. Sarah Sahara sells extraordinary information to very enterprising executives."

MONOCLE RELAY

This is a relay game, in which the teams line up single file, and the first person in each line places a quarter held over one eye, monocle style, and runs to a given point and back. No hands are allowed after the quarter is in place. If a player drops the quarter, he must come back and start over. The first team to finish is the winner. To make this one really tough, try it with two quarters, one in each eye.

NEWSPAPER RELAY

Teams line up on one end of the room. On the other end, hang the front page of the newspaper, or several clippings, or a whole newspaper. Prepare questions on the news stories ahead of time. You may ask questions and one person from each team runs to the newspaper and locates the correct answer, and the first to shout it out wins.

NO-CAN-SEE RELAY

Place two chairs fifty feet apart and place six cans of different sizes on the floor between the chairs. Two players are assigned one of the two chairs as a goal and are blindfolded. The object is for each player to place three cans, one at a time, under his chair. He can steal them from the opponent, or if he runs into the other player, he may take his can if he hits it with his hand. Be sure to indicate a time limit. The one with the most cans wins.

PING-PONG BALL FLOAT

For this relay, you will need coffee cans (empty), Ping-Pong balls, buckets of water, towels, and one fellow with his shirt off for every team participating.

The guy with his shirt off lies on his back about ten yards from his team who are in a single-file line. Place the coffee can (empty) on his stomach or chest. Put the Ping-Pong ball in the coffee can. A bucket full of water goes beside each team.

As the game begins, players use their cupped hands to carry water from their bucket to the coffee can. Each player goes one at a time. As the coffee can fills with water, the Ping-Pong ball rises in the can. As soon as it is high enough, a player tries to remove it from the can with his mouth. The first team to get the Ping-Pong ball out of the can (no hands) and back across the finish line, wins.

RACING SLICKS RELAY

This is a good outdoor game for camps, picnics, etc. Teams form straight lines. First person is given a twenty-five pound of ice. The object is to ride the ice down a grassy slope and carry it back. Arms and legs may be used for propulsion. All members of the winning team are awarded an ice cube.

REFRIGERATOR BOX RELAY

Mark off a large square. Divide group into four teams and

position a team at each corner of the square. Obtain four large refrigerator boxes and put one on each corner. This is a relay and the object is for one person from each team to put on a refrigerator box and walk to the opposite corner where the next person puts on the box and does the same. Fellow team members shout directions to the one in the box since he cannot see. First set of teams to get all their players across is the winner. When four walking boxes all meet in the center of the square at full speed, and none can see where they are going, you can imagine the results!

ROLLER-SKATE RUMBLE

Locate two pairs of roller-skates — the type that clamp on to your shoes (most kids have a pair). Be sure to get two skate keys also. Divide your group into two teams and then split each team in half. Half the team is at one end of the gym (or parking lot, etc.) and the other half is at the other end facing them. Team 2 does likewise!

On the signal to "go," the first person must put on the skates *tightly* (if they come off in mid-course, he must return and start all over!) and skate to the other side. He then takes the skates off (unaided) and hands to first person in line. The process continues relay-fashion until everyone has completed the course. First team to finish wins.

To make it even more interesting, we required all boys to skate across with their hands on their feet!

RUBBER BAND RELAY

Use three fellows in this "face-coordination" test. Place a rubber band around each player's head with it crossing over the tip of his nose. The idea, then, is to maneuver the rubber band from the nose down to the neck without using hands. Any facial contortion he can think of is legal.

SHAVING RELAY

Kids are divided into teams and each team is arranged girl-boy, girl-boy, etc. Each boy is given a balloon. The first girl of each team is given a can of shaving cream and a razor minus blade. At the signal of go the first boy blows up his balloon, ties it, and places it under his chin. The girl covers it with shaving cream and then shaves it. When finished, she passes the razor and shaving cream to the next girl. The second boy blows up his balloon, etc. First team to finish wins.

SKIPROPE-ISSY-DISSY RELAY

Each member of the team skips rope from starting line to a designated point where he puts down the rope and picks up a bat. He puts the small end of the bat to his forehead and with the large end on the ground spins around five times. He then picks up the skip rope and attempts to skip back to the starting line.

SOCK RELAY

Each participant is blindfolded and seated in a small circle within reach of a huge pile of worn-out socks. Each participant is given a pair of thick gloves to put on. On the signal, each participant tries to put as many socks on his feet as possible in the time allowed (about two minutes).

SOCK TAIL RELAY

Make several "sock tails," one for each team. A sock tail consists of a belt with a sock tied onto it, with an orange in the end of the sock as a weight. The first person on each team puts on the tail with the sock hanging down from behind. Another orange is placed on the floor. On the signal, the player must push the orange on the floor to a goal and back, with the sock tail. If he touches it with his feet or hands, he must start over. First team to have all team members complete this task wins.

SPOON RELAY

Divide the group into two lines, with a spoon in each player's mouth. The leader will place a marble in the spoon of each of the players at the head of the line and they will pass it from spoon to spoon until it reaches the end of the line. The group who reaches the end of their line first will be the winner. If the marble is dropped on its way to the end of the line, it must be started all over again.

SLEEPING BAG RELAY

Teams of equal number line up in single file. Each line is given one zipped-up sleeping bag. On signal the first person in line puts the sleeping bag over his head and is spun around three times. He then proceeds to run (stagger and stumble) to the opposite line. Audience and team members may cheer to assist staggerer to find right way, but they may not touch him. When he crosses the end line, he removes the bag and runs back, carrying the bag with him. Next person in line takes his turn. This continues until the team completes all turns. The first team finished is the winner.

STILTS RELAY

Have someone who is handy with wood make up four pairs of stilts out of 2x2's (two pairs for each team). The foot-mount should be 12-18 inches off the ground. Most players will be able to walk on them with ease. Just line the teams up relay style and let them go. The first team to go to the goal and back on stilts (one at a time) wins.

STRIPPER RELAY

This is a great game for swimming parties and "water carnivals." Get two or more teams of an equal number of participants. Obtain some baggy clothes (the funnier the better) for each team. Make sure that each team has similar clothing: shirts with buttons, pants with zippers, etc., to insure fairness during the relay. Place the clothes in individual team piles about twenty yards from the starting line on a raft or at the end of a pool. At the starting signal, one member of each team swims to the raft or end of the pool, climbs out of the water, puts the clothes on, strips the clothes off, and swims back to his team. He touches the next member of the team who then swims through the same process. First team to finish process wins.

SUCKER RELAY

Teams line up. Each person has a paper straw. A piece of paper (about 4 inches square) is picked up by sucking on the

straw and is carried around a goal and back. If you drop the
paper, you must start over. Each person on the team must do
it. First team to finish wins.

SUPER SACK RELAY

Divide into teams with 10 people on each team. Have a
brown paper bag for each team with the following items in
each:

> Jar of baby food
> Green onion
> Can of cola (warm)
> Raw carrot
> Piece of cream cheese (wrapped in wax paper)
> Box of Cracker Jacks
> Peanut butter sandwich
> An orange
> An apple
> A banana

On signal, the first member of each team runs to his bag and
must eat the first item he pulls out. Sponsors should make sure
items are satisfactorily finished before the person goes back
and tags the next member of the team. First team to finish its
sack wins.

TP RIP RELAY

This is a good game for camps or outdoor events, although it
may be used indoors. Each team selects four players to participate in this relay of skill. One guy walks backward toward a goal
some 50 feet away, unrolling a roll of toilet paper. Another one
follows him with a pair of scissors and cuts the roll in half,
lengthwise, without breaking the TP anywhere. Two more
players follow him, each cutting the two halves in half. The first

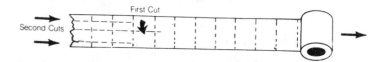

team to reach the goal and have four separate thin rolls of toilet paper, wins.

TELEPHONE GOSSIP RELAY

Make "phones" out of tin cans and string (see illustration) and play the "gossip game." One person gets on one end of the line and gives a message (one sentence) to the first person who listens with the can at his ear. The listener then runs to the other phone and relays the same message to the next team member who is now the listener. This continues until all the team has received the message. The last person on each team writes down the message he received. The closest to the original (in the fastest time) wins.

Hole punched in the end of each can

string pulled taut between cans

Knots shoud be tied in each end of string

THIMBLE RELAY

The teams form a line, and each player has a straw, which he holds upright in his mouth. The relay is started by placing the thimble on the straw held by the first person in line. It is then passed from player to player by means of the straw. The team to get the thimble to the end of the line first is the winner.

TOILET PAPER RELAY

Have each team line up single file and unwind a roll of TP over their heads when the signal is given. Each team continues to unwind the roll up and down the line until it is completely unrolled. First team to use up the entire roll wins.

WADDLE WALK RELAY

Have each team choose four people. Two of the four line up ten feet from the other two facing them. The object is to balance a cup of water on the head and walk with a balloon filled with air between the knees for the prescribed distance. If either the water or balloon fall, the person must start over. The first team to have all four contestants finish wins.

WATER BALLOON RELAY

Use as many couples as you want. Each couple races between two points holding a water balloon between their foreheads. Of course, the couples are facing each other and walk sideways. They cannot use their hands to hold the balloon. If the balloon drops, the couple picks it up and keeps going. If it breaks, they are out of the game.

ELIMINATION GAMES

ELIMINATION GAMES

AMERICAN EAGLE

This is not a co-ed game. Guys and gals should play separately. All players form a line. They choose one who stands 30 feet or so away (in the middle of a field). When the whistle is blown, players start running toward the one in the middle of the field. That person tackles one (or more if he can), and has to hold him down and say "American Eagle" three times. The rest of the players now are on the other side of the field, and now must run through two guys to get back to the original side again. This keeps up until everyone has been tackled and all are in the middle of the field. There are no more guys to run across. Give a prize to whomever lasts the longest.

ANATOMY SHUFFLE

This game is similar to "Birdie on the Perch." The group pairs off and forms two circles, one inside the other. One member of each couple is in the inside circle, the other is in the outside circle.

The other circle begins traveling in one direction (clockwise), and the inner circle goes in the opposite direction (counter-clockwise). The leader blows a whistle and yells out something like "Hand, Ear!" On this signal, each member of the inner circle group must find his partner and place his hand on the partner's ear. Last couple to do so is out of the game. The leader calls out all sorts of combinations as the game progresses, such as:

"Finger, Foot"	"Nose, shoulder"
"Thigh, Thigh"	"Head, stomach"
"Elbow, nose"	"Nose, Armpit"

The first thing called is always the inner group's part of the body, and the members of this group must find their partners, who stand in one position (they cannot move after the whistle blows) and touch their part of the body to the second item called on the partner. The last couple to remain in the game wins.

APPLE PARING RACE

Have several players race to see who can peel the longest continuous strip of peel off of an apple with a paring knife. Give the winner a sack of apples or a jug of cider.

BALLOON GOLF

This game is great in a small game room, and may also be played outdoors when there is no wind. First, drop a penny or smooth rock into each round balloon. Then blow the balloon up to about a 5 or 6-inch diameter. Golf clubs may be made by rolling a full sheet of newspaper into a stick. Cardboard boxes are used as the holes, with the par for each hole written on the side of the box. The weight inside the balloon creates a kind of Mexican jumping bean effect, causing both difficulty and hilarity for the participants.

BALLOON SMASH

Each person ties a balloon (blown up) around his waist so that the balloon hangs from his back. Each person also receives a rolled-up newspaper. Object is to break everyone else's balloon and keep your own from being broken. Newspapers are the only weapons allowed. Last surviving balloon wins.

BALLOON STOMP

Everyone receives a balloon and a piece of string. Each person blows up the balloon and ties it to his or her ankle with the string. When the game begins, kids try to stomp and pop everyone else's balloon while trying to keep their own intact. The last person with a balloon wins.

BARNYARD

Give each person a folded piece of paper with the name of an animal written on it. The person is not to say a word or look at the paper. He is to sit down and wait for further instructions. (To insure equal teams assign the same team every 6th person.) After everyone is in and seated, the group is told to look at their team name and when the lights are turned out they are to immediately stand up and make the sound of their animal:

1. Pig
2. Horse
3. Cow
4. Chicken
5. Duck
6. Dog

As soon as they find someone else who is making the same noise, they lock arms and try to find more of their teammates. When the lights come back on, everyone sits down. The team most "together" wins. For added fun, give *one* guy in the crowd the word "donkey" on his slip of paper. He'll wander around looking for more donkeys without any luck at all.

BIRDIE ON THE PERCH

Have players pair off and get into two concentric circles. If they are boy-girl couples, then the boys should be in the outside circle and the girls should be in the inside circle.

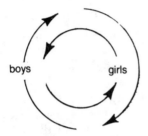

When the whistle blows, the boys circle begins moving clockwise and the girls circle moves counter-clockwise. When the leader yells "Birdie on the Perch!", the boys stop where they are and get down on one knee. The girls must quickly locate their partner and sit on his knee that is extended and put her arms around his neck. The last couple to get into that position is eliminated. The game continues until only one couple remains.

BIRTH DATE TURNOVER

This game is similar to the old game "Fruit Basket Turnover." Have everyone sit in a circle with the same number of chairs as there are people. "It" stands in the center, without a chair. He calls out any *three* months of the year. After the last month is called, everyone who has a birthday during one of those three months gets up and tries to take another seat. "It" also tries to find a vacant seat. Whoever is left without a seat becomes "it." The big move is when "It" calls "Leap Year." *Everyone* has to get up and find another seat.

CHAIR ROULETTE

This is simply musical chairs for big boys. Have 5 or 6 big players walk around chairs (one less than the number of walkers). Leader yells "stop!" and they grab a chair and sit down. Whoever is left without a chair is out. Remove one chair and do it again. Two players finally fight over one chair. Winner gets a prize.

CINDERELLA

Arrange chairs in a circle. All the Cinderellas (girls) in the group select a chair. The Prince Charmings (guys) each pick a Cinderella and kneel down in front of her. He removes her shoes and holds them in his hand. The leader calls for the shoes and they are thrown to the middle of the circle. Then the Cinderellas blindfold their Prince Charmings. After each prince is blindfolded, the leader rearranges and mixes the shoes in the middle. On a signal, all the Prince Charmings crawl to the circle and attempt to find their Cinderella's shoes. The Cinderellas can help only verbally, shouting out instructions to their men. After finding the shoes, the Princes crawl back to their girls (again guided only by verval instructions). They place the shoes (right one on right foot, etc.) on the girls and then remove their blindfolds. The game continues until the last contestant succeeds.

CLOTHESPIN PINUP

Here's a wild game that is simple, yet fun to play with any size group. Give everyone in the group six clothespins. On "go," each player tries to pin his clothespins on the other players' clothing. Each of your six pins must be hung on six different players. You must keep moving to avoid having clothespins hung on you, yet you try to hang your pins on someone else. When you hang all six of your clothespins, you remain in the game, but try to avoid having more pins hung on you. At the end of a time limit, the person with the smallest number of clothespins hanging on him (or her) is the winner and the person with the most is the loser.

Another way to play this game is to divide the group into pairs and give each person six clothespins. Each person then tries to hang all his pins on his partner. The winners then pair off again, and so on until there is a champion clothespinner.

CLUMPS

This game may be used for as many as 1000. Everyone crowds to the center with arms at sides. They are instructed to keep moving, but crowd toward the center. They must keep their arms at their sides. The leader blows a whistle or fog horn to stop all movement, and immediately yells out a number. If the number is 4, for instance, everyone must get into groups of 4, lock arms, and sit down. Leaders then eliminate all those not in groups of 4. This process is repeated, with different numbers each time, until all have been eliminated.

COTTONTAIL TAG

Have all the people in the group bring a can of shaving cream to the meeting. When the players show up you give each a "Bull's-eye Belt." This consists of a square foot of cardboard with a circle drawn on it and a string strung through it big enough to go around a player's waist. Each one ties it on his belt with the cardboard around back in the general area that a tail would go. You split the group into two teams and explain that the object of the game is to try and squirt a glob of shaving cream into the "Bull's-Eye" worn by members of the opposing team, while protecting yours at the same time. You may not touch your own or sit down on it. The shaving cream must stick to the cardboard and be inside the circle. The team that has successfully put the most "cotton tails" on the other team within the time limit is the winner.

DROP THE KEYS

Have the group sit in a circle facing inward. "It" is chairless and his object is to get a chair. This is accomplished by running quickly around the circle and grabbing the hand of someone of the opposite sex. The person whose hand was grabbed grabs someone else's hand (again, of the opposite sex). This continues as they are running around the circle (boy, girl, boy, girl). As the line gets longer, "it" goes under arms and between people to thoroughly tie the line in knots. All the while, the last person is still attempting to reach out and grab another person's hand sitting in the circle. When "it" chooses he drops the set of keys he has been carrying and everyone makes a mad dash for a chair.

EGG WALK

Lay eggs all over the floor and then blindfold a boy or girl and have them walk across the room without stepping on any. Substitute peanuts for the eggs after they are blindfolded. Put plenty of peanuts around and watch them scream.

ELEPHANT, RHINO, AND RABBIT

The players sit in a tight circle with "it" in the middle. "It" points to someone in the circle and says either "Elephant," "Rhino," or "Rabbit." The person to whom he points must either put his hands together in front of his nose for the "Elephant" or he must put both fists on his nose with the two index fingers pointing upward for the "Rhino." For "Rabbit" he must put index fingers pointing upward on each side of his head. The two people on either side of the player pointed to must put an open hand facing "it" to the first player's head for "Elephant." For "Rhino" they must put a fist to the person's head. For "Rabbit" they must put a fist to the head with one finger pointing upward. All of this must be done before the count of ten. If any one of the three people fails to do his part, he then becomes "it."

FICKLE FEATHER

Place a sheet out flat on the floor. Have all the players kneel around the sheet on all four sides of it, and then pick up the sheet by the edges. Then pull it taut and hold it under their chins. A feather is placed on the sheet, and the players try to blow the feather away from their side. Each side of the sheet is a team, and if the feather touches one of the team members, or gets blown over their heads, that team gets a point. The team with the fewest points is the winner.

FLEA MARKET

This is a good party game. You will need to prepare ahead of time a large number of one-inch square pieces of paper, all different colors. These are hidden all around the room. Some squares have numbers on them. On a starting signal, all members of the group hunt for the squares and then trade them with each other, trying to acquire the colors which they think are worth the most. (Only you know the color value.) The value of the colors and numbers is unknown to the players until the trading is over. You then announce the values and whoever has the most points, wins.

Colors: White = 1 point
                Brown = 5 points
                Green= minus 5 points
                Blue = 2 points
                Red = 10 points

Numbers: 7 = add 50
                11 = double score
                13 = subtract 50
                15 = add 1
                etc.

FRUITBASKET UPSET

This game may be played with any number of people, usually indoors. The entire group sits in an approximate circle with one less chair than there are people. The extra person stands in the middle. Everyone is secretly assigned the name of a fruit. The person in the middle begins by calling out several of the fruits. After naming several fruits, he yells, "Go," and those people who were assigned the fruits called must change chairs. At the same time, the person in the middle also tries to get one of the vacant chairs. The person who fails to get a chair is then the one in the middle and repeats the process. As an option, the person in the middle may call out "Fruitbasket Upset" at which time everyone must exchange chairs. Be sure to use sturdy chairs as this game is really wild and results in people landing in other people's laps, etc.

GUM SCULPTURE

Everyone is given equal amount of gum to chew. Each player is then given a 4 x 6 note card and a toothpick. Players must sculpture anything they want in a given time. The best sculpture is awarded a prize.

HOMEMADE GOLF

Use the inside of a large home and design a nine-hole minia- ture golf course using cans, cardboard, wood and anything else you can find. Make the course look interesting as well as fun to play. All you need is a package of light plastic golf balls, a few borrowed putters, odds and ends for the course and a little ingenuity. Use the whole youth group to design and make the course.

JACK AND THE BEANSTALK

Arrange chairs in a circle with enough room between them to allow each person to run around his chair. Leader goes around the circle and quietly assigns each person a character or object from the story and the corresponding sound (e.g. Jack's mother would say, "Jack, Jack, Jack" in falsetto, the giant says, "fe fi, fo, fum," clouds say, "puff, puff, puff," and on occasion you can make the real hams be the giant's commode saying, "flush, flush, flush.") For large groups it adds to the game to have the same characters on several sides of the circle. The leader then places someone out in the center and assigns him to be Jack. The leader then begins telling the story. As he comes to a part and mentions it, that person must go around his chair without touching it — making the assigned noise and sit down before "Jack" can come from the center and sit down in his chair. Anytime the leader says, "Beanstalk," everyone must move to a chair other than the ones on either side of him. After going through the story about halfway, the leaders should tell everyone they're going to shift into "spasm speed" and start telling the story as rapidly as possible.

JOHN - JOHN

This may be used for groups of up to 500. Form a circle using everyone. Selected leaders start the game by running to a person of opposite sex and yelling, "What's your name?" The person replies, "Linda." The leader looks behind himself and yells, "Linda — Linda . . . Linda — Linda — Linda" while doing a little dance similar to Mexican Hat Dance. The person (Linda in this case) falls in behind the leader, putting her hands on his waist, and together they run to the opposite side of the circle. This time they both do the above together. After they finish the little dance, Linda makes an about face. The leader does the same and grabs on to Linda's waist. The new person grabs on to the previous leader's waist. Now all three proceed to the opposite side of the circle with Linda leading. She should go to a boy. Each chain continues to get longer until everyone is chosen. There should be many chains and the object is to keep from getting hit by the other chains.

JOUSTING

This is a great game for camps or outdoor events. Construct jousting poles by using 2 x 2's about 12 feet long, and attaching padding to one end. The padding should be firmly in place, and should be soft. Foam rubber covered with towels and plenty of fabric tape has been found to be the best. Two boys challenge each other and each takes a jousting pole. The two must stand on a 2 x 4 on the ground or over a swimming pool and try to knock the other one off with jabs from his pole. You can't swing the pole, only jab with it.

KING OF THE CIRCLE

Mark off a big circle (10 feet or so in diameter) and put about a dozen men into it. At a signal each guy tries to throw everyone else out of the circle, and tries to stay in himself. Last one to stay in, wins.

LEMON GOLF

Kids get a broom and a lemon. They must hit the lemon with the stick end of the broom onto a piece of paper some distance away. It must stop on the piece of paper. Count the strokes as in regular golf.

LETTER SCRAMBLE

Before your next meeting, tape a letter (of the alphabet) to the bottom of every chair in the room. When the group sits down have everyone get his letter. You call out a word, and the first group of players to form the word, holding up their letters and standing in order in front of the group, gets a prize. (Note: Your "prize" can identify with the word you use, such as a package of "Certs" for the word "Halitosis.")

LINE PULL

Divide the group into two equal teams. The teams then face each other, by lining up on two sides of a line drawn on the floor. The object of the game is to pull the other team onto your side of the line. You cannot move behind your side of the line farther than three feet, and you must try to reach out and grab someone on the other side of the line without stepping over the line. Once you are over the line, you are automatically a member of that team and then you must try to help pull your former team over the line. At the end of the time period, the team with the largest number wins.

MATCH GAME

This is an indoor game that is quite simple and easy to play. Distribute a list similar to the following to each person:

1. Donut	14. Glass of water
2. The colonel	15. A place for reflection
3. A famous band	16. The reigning favorite
4. Looks like a foot	17. A morning caller
5. Headquarters	18. Seen at the ball game
6. A stirring event	19. Messenger
7. The end of winter	20. Fire when ready
8. A pair of slippers	21. Drive through the wood
9. Pig's retreat	22. Bound to shine
10. An old beau of mine	23. Life of China
11. The peace maker	24. Top dog
12. There love is found	25. My native land
13. Cause of the Revolution	

Next, place various articles on a table or around the room that will match the "clues" given in the first list. For example, the corresponding items for the preceding list would be:

1. The letter "o" on a card	5. Pillow
2. Kernel of corn	6. Spoon
3. Rubber band	7. Letter "r"
4. Ruler	8. Two banana peels

 9. Writing pen
10. Old ribbon bow
11. Pair of scissors
12. Dictionary
13. Tacks on tea bags
14. Blotter or sponge
15. Mirror
16. Umbrella
17. Alarm clock

18. Pitcher
19. Penny (one sent)
20. Match
21. Nail
22. Shoe polish
23. Rice
24. Hot dog
25. Dirt

Of course, you may think of many more besides these. The winner is the person who can correctly match up all the items in the shortest time. To make the game harder, place twice as many items on the table than you have clues for.

MOTHER GOOSE PAIRS

As each guest arrives, he is given a "Mother Goose" character or object and another youth is given a name taken from the same rhyme. The object is for the two characters from the same rhyme to locate each other without using questions or answers, but only sound effects and actions. For example, the boy falling off the stool and the marching soldier should soon get together as "Humpty Dumpty" and the "Kings Men."

MUD SLIDE

Why let rain ruin camp? Grass is very slick when it's wet. Pick the steepest convenient and acceptable grassy slope and let the kids slide down with or without plastic toboggans or cardboard. Presently the grass will give out and you'll have a nice mudslide.

MUSICAL HATS

Pick six boys to stand in a circle, each facing the back of the boy in front. In other words, they would all be looking clockwise, or all counterclockwise. Five of the guys put on hats (or you can use paper paint buckets) and on a signal (or when the music starts) each guy grabs the hat on the person's head in front of him and puts it on his own head. That way, the hats are moving around the circle from head to head until the next signal (or when the music stops). At that point, whoever is left without a hat is out of the game. Remove one hat and do it again until there are only two guys left. They stand back to back, grabbing the hat from each others' head, and when the final signal is given, the one with the hat on is the winner.

NOODLE WHOMP

First have two girls get down on all fours, facing each other, with blindfolds on. They should join left hands. Each girl has a rolled-up newspaper, and gets three tries to hit the other girl with it. The girl being swung at may move anywhere to try and get out of the way, but cannot move her left hand. Whichever girl gets hit the most times is the loser. Try it next with a pair of boys. Lastly, have a championship with the boy winner playing the girl winner. After the blindfolds are on, take the blindfold off the girl. The boy will get clobbered.

PAPER PLANES

Let everyone come up with his own paper airplane, made out of anything he wants, so long as it is paper. Give awards for the best designed airplane, the farthest flight, and the plane that stays in the air the longest. Players may use paint, glue, and paper, but may not use wire, wood, or metals.

PASS IT ON

The entire group forms a circle. Everyone is given an object which can be large, small or any shape (such as a bowling ball, a trash can, a shoe, etc.). On a signal, everyone passes his object to the person on the right, keeping the objects moving at all times. When a person drops any object, he must leave the game, but his object remains *in*. As the game progresses, more people leave the game, making it harder and harder to avoid dropping an object since there become more objects than people very quickly. The winner is the last person(s) to "drop" out.

PINCH ME

Here's a wild game great for dividing a large group into smaller groups. Everyone is to remain silent (no talking, but laughing, screaming, etc. is permitted). Each person receives a slip of paper which he is to keep secret from everyone else. The papers all read something like:

> Pinch Me
> Slap Me
> Tickle Me
> Step on My Toes
> Rub My Tummy
> Scratch My Back
> Pull My Ear

The lights are turned out, so it is dark. When everyone has a card, the leader yells "go" and the players must find the others in their group. For instance, a "Pinch Me" must go around pinching everyone until he finds someone else who is a "Pinch Me." They stick together pinching others until they find the rest of their team. There should be an equal number in each group. After a period of time, the leader stops the game, and the team with the largest number wins.

PLASTIC BOWL

Use plastic bottles for pins and a volleyball or similar ball for bowling. Works great for picnics and all-day game events.

POLE-ISH PILLOW FIGHTING

Get two guys to volunteer for a pillowfight. Tie (loosely) the end of a length of rope to each of two poles (such as basketball net poles or trees). Have the two volunteers standing between the poles about three feet apart and tie the other ends of the two ropes to the two guys. Explain to them that they will be blindfolded to fight and the ropes are to keep them slightly apart. They will know that when they are at the end of their rope the opponent is only three feet away, thus making it easier to locate him. Then blindfold them while they are still out in the middle. Tell them you are bringing each back to his pole to start. As you return each to his pole, have the person who tied the ropes to the poles draw in some of the rope and re-tie it. As the pillowfighters return to the center to fight they won't be able to reach each other. As they come out, you take a pillow, get between them in the middle, and beat them to death! (Let them hit you once or twice so they don't lose heart.)

POLISH PING-PONG

This game requires the same equipment as regulation Ping-Pong, and the game begins in the same way. But after the ball crosses the net on the serve, it must bounce at least once on the table and once on the floor before it can be returned. On the return serve, the ball has to hit the table once (it does not have to cross the net) and then bounce on the floor once before it may be returned. The ball on any return serve (once it is across the net in the beginning serve) and from then on, may bounce from 1 to 12 (or more) times on the table, but may only be hit after it has bounced once on the floor.

The fun begins, for example, when a returned serve hits the table on the return side, takes a quick bounce off to the left or right side of the table, and bounces on the floor. It's now up to the server to get to the ball and hit it back up on the table (anywhere) after the first bounce. Here, surprise shots can cause quite a mad scramble for the ball.

Fun also enters in when the table is in a room with close walls and a low ceiling. Then combination shots off the walls and ceiling add to the excitement. Here, the rule of one bounce is altered, as the ball can first bounce against the walls or ceiling before hitting the floor and after bouncing off the table, and it is still considered a "fair shot."

Also, a return server may hit the ball (after the floor bounce) against the wall, carrom it off the ceiling, hit the table on one or more bounces, and then continue to another wall or floor. It's then up to the other person to get that ball as soon as it leaves the first bounce on the floor. Again, quickness and practice pay off. There are some games in which all one does is run from one end of the table to the other just to keep in the game.

Score is kept in the same way as in regulation Ping-Pong: each server serves until 5 points are made (total) and after a total of 10 points the people switch sides. This is done since some room combinations favor one side or the other.

Increased fun will result when teams play with mandatory alternate shots on both teams. This causes real excitement as one team member is always in the other's way, or the person who is to return the serve is always on the wrong side of the table. Again, fast footwork and expert combination shots are the keys to success.

If in any game, after the first serve, the ball bounces on the table, hits the net and then goes off to the floor, it constitutes a "fair shot." Also any "net" ball on a return shot which causes the ball to stop dead on the table, may be blown off the table by the person who's next to hit it. However, he must wait till it bounces once off the floor before hitting it. A team member may blow it off for you to add suspense in team competition.

Typical Polish Ping-Pong Game

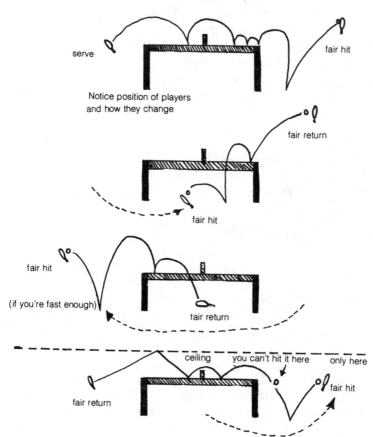

PULL-UP

Everyone gets a chair and forms a circle, everyone sitting in his chair and facing the center of the circle except for 5 boys and 5 girls who start the game. (They are in the middle, standing). At a whistle the 10 boys and girls in the center of the circle run to the people sitting in the chairs and "pull-up" a person of the opposite sex, by taking his hands and pulling him out of his chair. For example a boy would go up to a girl, pull her out of her chair and then *take her seat*. The girl may offer no resistance. She then runs to the other side of the circle, pulls a boy out of his chair, and takes his seat, etc. This continues for 30 seconds, the whistle blows, and everyone stops where he is. The boys and girls left standing are counted. If there are 2 more girls than boys, the boys get 2 points, and the game continues. Every half-minute, the whistle blows and those standing are counted. The idea is sort of a random "musical chairs," boys against the girls. The team with the least left standing each time wins.

RATTLESNAKE

For this game of stealth and skill, you will need two blindfolds, a small plastic bottle (a Rx bottle works fine) with a rock in it, and a defined area for play. This may be done on large mats (of the wrestling variety) or on a carpeted floor. The referee blindfolds both players and spins them around so that they lose their sense of direction. We are now ready to begin play. It is essential that everyone remains absolutely quiet (everyone not playing is seated around the edges of the playing area). The referee says, "Rattlesnake!" The rattlesnake must shake his "rattle" and then try to escape capture by the hunter. The game continues with the referee periodically saying, "Rattlesnake," until the hunter captures the rattlesnake.

ROUND BUZZARD

"Round Buzzard" is played with the same rules and the same way as a game called "Round Robin." In Round Robin, everyone stands in a circle around a Ping-Pong table. There is one Ping-Pong paddle on each end of the table and one Ping-Pong ball used in the game. It begins with one person serving the ball just as in a Ping-Pong game. But after he serves, he must rotate around the table and allow the person next to him to receive the return of his serve. In other words, you hit the ball, put the paddle down on the table, move to your right, out of the way, so the person next to you can pick up the paddle and return the ball from someone on the other end of the table.

Round Buzzard is played the exact same way, except for a few minor changes.

1. Instead of a Ping-Pong ball, use a tennis ball.

2. Instead of Ping-Pong paddles, use tennis rackets. (Old ones because they take a beating.)

3. Instead of playing on a Ping-Pong table, you play on a tennis court, or volleyball court.

The other rules for Round Buzzard are the same as for Round Robin. There is just a lot more running, especially near the end, when each person who either misses the ball (or fails to return the serve or keep the volley going) is *out of the game*, and there are only three or four people left. It requires a lot of hustle.

RUB MY BACK AND I'LL RUB YOURS

Everyone pairs off. Clip a number of clothespins on each person's back (the same number for each player). They should be clipped to shirt or coat tails, or wherever there is some loose clothing. On "go," the partners rub backs, and try to knock all the clothespins off without using hands. The first to do so is the winner.

SADIE HAWKINS RACE

Give each boy a piece of red yarn or ribbon and have him tie it around his ankle. At a signal, each girl tries to get a ribbon from a boy's ankle. If she succeeds, he is her partner for the next game. Don't play this in a room where something is breakable because it is really wild!

SCATTERBALL

How about an old game that is probably new for most young people today? Everyone is assigned a number with two mystery numbers not assigned to anyone else. The person who has the ball throws it up in the air and calls a number. Everyone scatters except the person whose number was called. He immediately retrieves the ball and yells, "Stop." He then tries to hit someone with the ball. Letters are given 1) if a person is hit with the ball and 2) if the throw misses everyone. Also, if a mystery number is called everyone gets a letter. People who get four letters, S-C-A-T, are eliminated.

SHOE KICK

Have boys take off one shoe, and hang it off the end of one foot. The idea is to see who can "kick" his shoe the farthest. You will be surprised to see how many guys wind up kicking their shoes over their heads, behind them, or straight up in the air.

SHOULDER PIN

Have two boys come to the front, sit on the floor back to back and lock arms. On a signal, they each try to pin the other's right shoulder to the floor. It is similar to Indian arm wrestling, only using your whole body.

SHOULDER TAG

Everyone puts his left arm behind his back, and grabs his ankles with his right hand. In this bent-over position, he hops or walks around and tries to knock the other players off balance. Anyone who falls down is out of the game. The last player to remain in is the winner. This is best as a "guys only" or a "girls only" game. Elbowing and butting with the shoulders is not allowed.

SHUFFLE YOUR BUNS

Arrange chairs in a circle so each person has a chair. There should be two extra chairs in the circle. Each person sits in a chair except for two people in the middle who try to sit in the two vacant chairs. The persons sitting in the chairs keep moving around from chair to chair to prevent the two in the middle from sitting down. If one or both of the two in the middle manage to sit in a chair, the person on their right replaces them in the middle of the circle and then tries to sit in an empty chair.

SING SONG SORTING

This game is similar to "Barnyard" and is great as a way to divide a crowd into teams or small groups. Prepare ahead of time on small slips of paper an equal number of four (or however many groups you want) different song titles. As each person enters the room, he receives (at random) one of these song titles. In other words, if you had 100 players and you wanted four teams, there would be 25 each of the four different songs. On a signal, the lights go out (if you do this at night) and each player starts singing the song he received as loudly as possible. No talking or yelling, only singing. Each person tries to locate others singing the same song, and the first team to get together is the winner. Song titles should be well-known.

SKUNK

This is a game of strength and agility. You need a defined padded area, either a carpeted floor, or a large mat. In the center of the playground, place a real skunk skin, or a reasonable substitute. Have players stand with locked arms over the skin. At the signal, "go," each tries to force the other to touch the skunk skin with some part of his body. The first one to touch the skin loses. Have the other people sit around the playing area to keep the sprawling players on the mat.

SNATCH

This is a good game for camps or outdoor events, and is best used with junior highers. Group is divided into two teams each lined up behind its goal line 20-30 feet apart. A handkerchief is placed at a point half-way between goal lines. Each player is given a number. The two teams are numbered from opposite ends of the line.

The leader calls out a number. The player on each team having that number runs to the center and tries to snatch the handkerchief and return to his goal without being tagged by the other one. The more skilled player will run into the center and hover over the handkerchief until such a time when he can snatch it and run when his opponent is off guard. Each successful return gains one point for the team. After each successful tag or score, the handkerchief is returned to the center and another number is called. Play for a designated number of points. The leader should call numbers in a manner to create suspense. All numbers should be included, but it is well to repeat a number now and then to keep all players alert. Also, maintain interest by calling two or more numbers simultaneously, thereby involving four or more players.

STACK 'EM UP

Have everyone sit in chairs in a circle. Prepare a list of qualifying characteristics such as those found in the "Sit Down Game." Here are a few examples:

1. If you forgot to use a deodorant today . . .

2. If you got a traffic ticket this year . . .

3. If you have a hole in your sock . . .

4. If you are afraid of the dark . . .

Then read them one at a time and add " . . . move three chairs to the right" or "move one chair to the left," etc. In other words, you might say, "If you forgot to use a deodorant today, *move three chairs to the right,*" and all those who "qualify" move as instructed and sit in that chair, regardless of whether or not it's occupied by one or more persons. As the game progresses, players begin "stacking up" on certain chairs.

STREETS AND ALLEYS

One person is "it" and chases another person through a maze of people formed in this manner:

Everyone in the maze is facing in one direction with hands joined, forming "alleys." When "streets" is called, all do a right face and grasp hands once more. The person who is "it" tries to catch the runner, and cannot cross the joined hands. When "alleys" is called, everyone in the maze assumes his original position, etc.

SWAT

Group sits in a circle in the center of which is a wastebasket turned bottom-up. One person is "it" and stands inside the circle with a rolled-up newspaper. "It" walks around the inside of the circle and swats one person's knee. He must then put the newspaper back on top of the wastebasket and return to the swatted person's seat before that person grabs the newspaper and hits "it." If the newspaper falls off the wastebasket, it must be put back.

SWIVEL HIPS

Have the group sit in a circle with chairs close together. A chosen person then stands up and the person on his right moves, and sits in his chair and the person on the right moves and sits in his chair, and as this continues the person who stands tries to get a seat. If the person is able to get a seat, the person whose seat was taken stands up and the circle continues to move.

Once the group has begun to master the movement, you can ask them to switch directions. To make it even more fun, blow a whistle to signal the change of direction. If you have a large group, you can have two or three people trying to find seats.

TARGET PRACTICE

Place a table against a wall. On the table place many "targets" made from paper folded in half. These targets should be various sizes from two inches to about six inches. Place point values on each one (10, 25, 50, 100) depending on how big the target is. Each team gets an "arsenal" of rubber bands and tries to shoot as many targets over in one minute as possible. All players must stand behind a line 15 feet (or so) away from the table. Points are scored each time a target is knocked over. Team with the most points wins.

TARP TOSS

Have manufactured by a tent or awning company a circular tarp, reinforced on the edges, with loops or special places for young people to hang on approximately shoulder to shoulder around the circumference of the tarp. The idea is to take a young person, place him in the center of the tarp, then all of the young people around the edge pull evenly together. It has about the same effect as tossing someone into the air with a blanket. However, the tarp is much more resilient and a great deal like a trampoline. Tarp size may vary, but at least a 10' diameter is recommended.

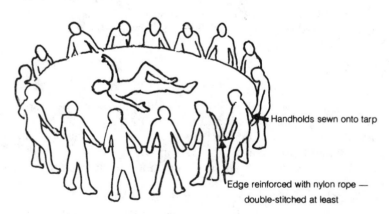

Handholds sewn onto tarp

Edge reinforced with nylon rope — double-stitched at least

TETHERBALL JUMP

Here's an old game that groups really enjoy. Have ten to twenty players form a circle. You get in the center of the circle with a tether ball (a ball attached to a rope about eight feet long). Take the rope in your hand and begin making circles with the ball, about six inches off the ground. The circle of players then moves in closer and each person must jump over the ball as it passes by. You keep going around and around, getting faster and faster until someone goofs. That person is then out, and the game continues. The last person to remain is the winner. As the game progresses, you may make the ball go faster and/or higher off the ground. Two leaders (ball twirlers) are recommended to take shifts in the center if you get dizzy easily.

THIRD DEGREE

The leader divides the group into two teams, one composed of FBI members, the other of spies. Each spy is given a card bearing one of the instructions listed below, each spy receiving a different instruction. The FBI members then take turns asking questions of specific spies, calling out the name of each spy before asking the question. The FBI members may ask as many questions of as many or as few spies as they decide, and may ask any questions they wish (except about the instructions the spies were given). Each spy must answer each question asked him, but always in the manner described on his card. Whenever a spy's instruction is guessed correctly by an FBI member, that spy is eliminated from the game. The questions continue until all the spies' instructions are guessed correctly. If a spy gives an answer without following his instructions, he is eliminated.

Scores are kept on individuals rather than teams. The winning spy is the one who has the most questions asked him before his instructions are guessed correctly. The winning FBI member is the one who guesses correctly the most number of instructions. (An FBI member may make a guess at any time, whether it is his turn to ask a question or not.)

1. Lie during every answer.

2. Answer each question as though you were (name of leader).

3. Try to start an argument with each answer you give.

4. Always state the name of some color in each answer.

5. Always use a number in your answers.

6. Be evasive — never actually answer a question.

7. Always answer a question with a question.

8. Always exaggerate your answers.

9. Always pretend to misunderstand the question by your answer.

10. Always scratch during your answers.

11. Always insult the questioner.

12. Always begin each answer with a cough.

13. Always mention some kind of food during each answer.

14. Always mention the name of a group member during your answers.

THIS LITTLE LIGHT

This game is very similar to Barnyard. Each person is given a flashlight (or brings one) and a special code (one flash, two flashes, one long and one short flash, etc.). The number of teams desired determines the number of codes. As soon as all the codes are assigned, turn out the lights. The kids are to group together by finding all others using similar codes.

TONGUE-TIE

Have three fellows come up to the front and each is given a piece of wrapped bubble gum. On a signal, each player puts the gum in his mouth, wrapper and all, and must unwrap the gum in his mouth (no hands), spit the wrapper out, chew the gum, and then blow a bubble. First one to do so wins a prize.

TOWEL THROW

This is a simple but exciting game for small groups. The group is seated in chairs preferably in a closed circle. One person stands inside the circle. The group passes or throws a towel around the circle (to anyone in the circle they choose). The person in the middle then tries to tag the person who has the towel. When he catches someone with the towel, the two exchange positions. Also, if he catches the towel in mid-air, the one who threw it has to exchange positions and become "it," and the game is resumed.

TRAIN WRECK

Arrange chairs in a straight line with an aisle down the middle. Each person, including the "conductor," is numbered and sits in a chair. The conductor stands in front and calls out seven numbers (not his own). He then yells, "Train wreck!" The people with the numbers called must exchange seats with each other (it doesn't matter which one as long as it is not your own). The conductor tries to find an empty seat. The person without a chair is the new conductor.

TURTLE RACE

Cut a number of turtle shapes out of thin plywood similar to the diagram below. Make sure that all the shapes are identical. Drill a hole in the neck. Thread a heavy string through the hole and tie one end to a fixed object.

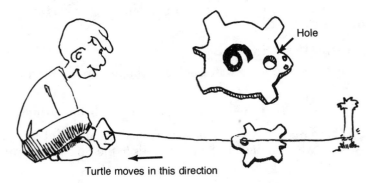

Turtle moves in this direction

When the string is pulled upward, the turtle lifts up and scoots forward. The legs must always stay touching the floor. The higher the turtle is lifted, the further it will scoot. But look out! . . . you are liable to flip him over and lose ground while your opponents are in hot pursuit. For relays, have someone at each end of the string (one holding and one pulling). When the turtle reaches a certain finish line, flip him over and the other teammate takes him back. This game is a great crowd-pleaser.

TWISTER

This game is available at most toy or party stores. Manufactured by the Milton Bradley Company, it consists of a plastic mat with colored spots on it, and a "spinner" which determines what the players must do. For example, the spinner might say, "left hand, yellow," which means a player must put his left hand on a yellow spot on the mat. The next player spins and might come up with "right foot, red," meaning he must put his right foot on a red spot, and so on. As the game progresses, the players are forced to become contortionists, and get into some unbelievable positions. The first person to fall over (lose his balance) is the loser.

UNDERDOG

Choose one player to be "it." "It" tags the free players, who must "freeze" when tagged. Frozen players must obtain freedom by spreading their legs apart, allowing a free player to pass between their open legs. "It" must freeze all the free players and the game is over. Spice up the game by making two or three players "it."

WATERMELON GAMES

Next time you serve watermelon to your group, try these fun games.

1. *Seed Spit-off:* See who can spit his seeds the farthest.

2. *Seed Race:* Give each player an equal size slice and race to see who can dig out the most seeds in the time limit — or out of his piece.

3. *Watermelon Carving:* Players carve creative designs with a knife out of the watermelon rind.

WATER PONG

Fill two small saucers or shallow bowls full of water and place one on each side of the Ping-Pong net about twelve inches from the net and on the center line. If your opponent can drop or hit the ball (in regular playing rules) in your saucer, he wins the game. Score the game normally unless the ball lands in the saucer.

YARN GUESS

This is one of those things you do just for fun. On one side of the room, put some numbers on the wall (on cards or just write on the wall). Attach to the number the end of a long piece of yarn. Then hang the yarn up the wall, across the ceiling, and down the opposite wall to a letter on the wall. Let the yarn make a few turns, go through things, etc., to make it interesting. With about 25 different lengths of yarn going across the room connecting numbers and letters, it really looks wild. The object is to have the players try to figure out which number connects with which letter. Whoever guesses the most right wins a prize.

SPECIAL EVENTS

SPECIAL EVENTS

AUTUMN MADNESS

This event is similar to the popular table-top game called "Clue." However, instead of using a game board, you use your whole city (or neighborhood, church, camp, or wherever you choose to locate the event). The event is called "Autumn Madness," simply because the originators of it held the event in autumn. But you can call it anything you want.

The object of the game:

A murder has been committed by one of ten suspects. It is known that the murderer used one of ten weapons and committed the crime in one of ten rooms in the victim's house on one of seven days of the week. It is also known that his motive for killing the victim was one of ten reasons. (A total of 47 possibilities.)

Each person will attempt to determine the suspect, the weapon, the motive, the room and the day of the murder. To do this, each person must use a process of elimination to cut down the number of possibilities to be considered. This is done in two ways: (1) By asking the suspects simple yes or no questions and (2) by accumulating "clue card quarters." (When properly matched, four clue card quarters will form an entire clue which will eliminate one of the possibilities.)

The suspects are located in houses or buildings all over the city and the players in the game must travel to these locations as they question the suspects. (If you confine the game to a camp, the suspects may be located in different cabins; if you use one large building, such as a church, then the suspects may be located in different rooms.) The suspects may be sponsors, staff, or complete strangers to the group. There may be more than one suspect at each location.

Each player receives:

1. A clue sheet listing all the suspects, weapons, motives, rooms, and days to choose from. It is to be used as a worksheet as information is gathered.

Suspects	Weapons	Motives	Rooms	Days
Maid	Knife	Money	Hall	Sunday
Milkman	Candlestick	Passion	Lounge	Monday
Playboy	Gun	Jealousy	Dining Room	Tuesday
Gardener	Rope	Power	Kitchen	Wednesday
Movie Star	Lead Pipe	Amusement	Ballroom	Thursday
Old Lady	Wrench	Accident	Closet	Friday
Farmer	Meat Cleaver	Greed	Library	Saturday
Butler	Hatchet	Hatred	Bathroom	
Singer	Poison	Fear	Parlor	
Magician	Shovel	Insanity	Garage	

2. A map showing the location of each suspect. (This point is irrelevant to the game, but is helpful.)

3. Four clue card quarters are received at each location. The first four are given out at the start of the game.

4. An accusation slip and envelope. When a person is ready to make a final guess at solving the mystery, the accusation slip is filled out, signed, sealed in the envelope, and handed to one of the suspects (any one). The time is recorded (to the second) on the outside of the envelope when the suspect receives it, and the first correct guess is the winner. All the envelopes will be opened at the "Mad Hatter's Tea Party," following the game. Once a person guesses, he is out of the game, and goes directly to the site of the "tea party."

How the game is played:

Each person is on his own. If players travel in carloads, they should not give information to each other freely. Information may be traded, however, to any person's best advantage. Players should be encouraged to come up with a strategy for information swapping, otherwise they may wind up hurting their own cause.

Players may ask each suspect two questions which can be answered with a "yes" or "no," such as, "Was the murder weapon a knife?" If the suspect knows, he will answer "yes" or "no." If he does not know, he will answer "I don't know." Each suspect only has information about one of the five items to be determined. No suspect may be questioned a second time until all the suspects have been questioned once. Each person should be allowed to question suspects alone. If this is a problem, then players should write their questions down and give them to each suspect.

At each location, players will receive a new "clue card quarter." When a matching set of "clue card quarters" fit together, the finished clue should look like this:

Butler 1	Butler 7
Butler 3	Butler 4

If the total of the four numbers on the clue is *even*, then the answer is "yes"; if the total is *odd*, the answer is "no." For example, the clue above would say "No, the butler is not the suspect," because the total is 15, an odd number. Clue card quarters may be traded with other players.

The winner is the first to correctly identify each of the five parts of the mystery. At the "grand opening" of the accusations the envelopes with the earliest time written on the envelope are opened first.

The key to the game is asking the right questions to the right

suspects. Some questions will be lucky guesses, but by determining who knows what, a player can be much more precise in
his questioning process.

A time limit should be set at which time everyone must make
a guess at the five items. The accusation slips are filled out,
turned in, and the winners revealed. The accusation slips look
like this:

```
┌──────────────────────────────────────────────────────────────┐
│                                                              │
│                        Accusation Slip                       │
│                                                              │
│     The suspect who committed the crime is:                  │
│                                                              │
│     The weapon used was a:                                   │
│                                                              │
│     The motive for the murder was:                           │
│                                                              │
│     The room of the house was:                              │
│                                                              │
│     The day of the week was:                                 │
│                                                              │
└──────────────────────────────────────────────────────────────┘
```

Award everyone who guessed all five correctly a consolation
prize of some kind, for a "job well done."

Each of the ten suspects should be instructed to give information on only one of the five items involved in the crime. That
means that two suspects will know who did it, two will know
the weapon, etc.

If you do use houses all over town for the locations of the
suspects, you might consider setting up a "shuttle service,"
with cars going from one location to another, making stops at
each one. After a player asks a suspect his questions, he then
waits for the next available shuttle to the next location.

BACKWARD NIGHT

This is a fun activity in which *everything* is done in reverse.
Invitations and posters should be printed backwards (even
from bottom to top), and oral announcements should be made
with your back to the audience.

As the people arrive, they should use the back door of the
church or meeting place. Appropriate signs, spelled backwards, could be placed at the regular entrance directing them
to the rear. Each person should come to this event with his
clothes on backwards, and inside-out.

Greet the guests at the door with "Good-by, hope you had a good time," and other such salutations, and the program should be run exactly in reverse. As the people leave, put name tags on them, welcome them, and introduce visitors. If paper plates are used for refreshments, use them upside down, and make everyone eat left-handed (if they are right-handed).

Divide the group into four teams (at least) for the following games. *Subtract* points for the winners, rather than awarding points. (Have each team begin with 10,000 points, then they lose points as they win.) The team names may be barnyard animals, and the team members must make the noise of their animal during the games. Only the sounds should be in reverse. For example, a donkey would go "Haw-hee," and a dog would go "Wow-Bow." A cow would go "Ooooom." Here are a few suggested games:

1. *Backward Charades:* This game is just like regular charades, only the titles must be acted out in reverse. For example, instead of "The Sound of Music," the player must act out "Music of Sound The." The team must correctly guess the backward title.

2, *Backward Letter Scramble:* Before the party prepare four sets of cards (one set for each team) with the letters B-A-C-K-W-A-R-D on them. In other words, each team gets eight cards, each with one of those eight letters written on it. The cards are passed out to the various team members. You then call out certain words that can be spelled using those letters, and the first team to get in line, spelling the word *backward*, is the winner. Words to use include: Backward, drab, rack, ward, raw, ark, back, crab, bark, etc. If you called out the word "drab," for example, the kids with those four letters must quickly line up facing you so that the cards spelled it "b-a-r-d."

3. *Relay* games: Use any of the relays from the books in this series,* but run backwards.

4. *Behind the Back Pass:* Teams line up shoulder to shoul-

Far-Out Ideas for Youth Groups, Right-On Ideas for Youth Groups, Way-Out Ideas for Youth Groups, by Mike Yaconelli and Wayne Rice, all published by Zondervan.

der. Several objects are then passed down the line from player to player, only behind their backs. The first team to pass a certain number of these objects all the way down the line is the winner. For fun, try using cups of water. Spilling is a penalty and points will be added to the score.

BACKWARDS PROGRESSIVE DINNER

This idea may be used in conjunction with the previous idea, "Backwards Night." It is a regular "progressive dinner" in which the participants travel from location to location, and receive one "course" of their meal at each stop. The fun with this one is that the menu is served in reverse. It would go something like the following:

Stop One: Dessert and a toothpick
Stop Two: Potato chips
Stop Three: Sandwich
Stop Four: Vegetable
Stop Five: Salad
Stop Six: Soup
Stop Seven: Appetizer

Have something to drink at each stop.

BANANA NIGHT

Here's a party idea that will cause your group to really "go bananas." The theme is bananas and many events can be planned using the popular yellow fruit:

1. *Banana Stories:* Give a prize for the best story or poem about bananas.

2. *Banana Costumes:* Give a prize for the best banana costume. Have everyone wear yellow and suggest that the kids make good use of those little stickers that come on bunches of bananas.

3. *Banana Prizes:* Award banana splits, "Bic Bananas" (the ballpoint pen), etc.

4. *Banana Relay:* A wild team game. (See "Relay Games.")

5. *Banana Race:* Each team gets a bunch of bananas with the same number of bananas in each. Teams line up with their bananas about 50 feet away. Each team member then runs to his team's bananas and eats one, returns, tags the next player and so on. The team to finish first wins.

BEAN-BAG BALL

This is a wild game great for camps and may be set up like a championship "football" game. Divide the crowd into two large groups and give them names of schools (make them up). Each "school" is then provided plenty of newspapers, tape, magic markers, crepe paper, scissors, poster paint, etc. They then have thirty minutes or so to do the following:

a) Prepare a band, complete with uniforms (make them), instruments (anything you can find), drum major, majorettes, etc., plus a march or two that can be hummed (waxed paper on combs help here). One band should be prepared to play the "Star Spangled Banner."

b) Prepare cheerleaders (usually boys dressed like girls), complete with costumes, cheers, etc.

c) Prepare a Homecoming Queen with court (could be boys or girls, or mixed). Fix up costumes.

d) Prepare a team for "Bean-Bag-Ball" (see following rules). Ordinarily a team of seven plus a coach will do.

e) Prepare a half-time program and a crowning of the Homecoming Queen and Court.

After each school has done all this, then begin the action as follows:

a) School A Marching Band marches onto the field followed by the team and cheerleaders. An announcer introduces the team. The cheerleaders do their stuff.

b) School B does the same.

c) Leaders ask one band to play the "Star Spangled Banner."

d) First half of the game (5 to 7 minutes), cheerleaders and bands do stuff.

e) Half-time program:
   - School A's program and crowning of Queen.
   - School B's program and crowning of Queen.

f) Second half of the game.

g) Victory celebration by the winning team.

Here's how "Bean-Bag-Ball" is played: Two referees are needed with whistles. The playing field may vary in size, but anything larger than a volleyball court will do. There should be a half-way line and at each end of the field a folding chair is placed three feet beyond the goal line. The rules are similar to basketball except the bagholder may only take three steps with the bean bag, then he must pass it. Goals are scored by tossing the bean bag between the seat and the seatback of the chair. A good P.A. system and announcer will add a great deal.

BICYCLE PEDALMONIUM DAY

This is a fun event that can involve everyone in the group in an exciting day full of bike activities. Divide the action into three separate parts: (1) A Bicycle Olympics, (2) A Bike Road Rally, and (3) A Bike Tour. Begin around noon on a Saturday (or a holiday) and run all the activities during the afternoon.

Bicycle Olympics:

Divide the crowd into four competing groups, by ages (junior high, high school, college). Points and prizes may be awarded the winners in each division. Some sample events:

1. *100 Yard Dash:* A race for time. Use a stopwatch.

2. *20-Lap Endurance Race:* Should be about five miles on a regular quarter-mile track. Award points to first through fifth places.

3. *Backward Race:* Should be optional. Players ride with their backs to the front tire.

4. *Figure Eight Race:* Set up a figure eight track and contestants ride it, one at a time, for best clocked time.

5. *Obstacle Race:* Set up a track with obstacles (mud, trees, or whatever) to make riding difficult.

6. *Bike Jousting:* Bike riders ride toward each other in parallel lanes. Each rider gets a water balloon. The object is to ride by your opponent and hit him with the balloon, without getting hit yourself. Winners advance to semifinals, finals, etc.

Bike Road Rally:

This is a simple "treasure hunt" event in which teams of three to four bike riders must follow clues to reach a final destination. By arranging for the teams to go different routes, yet ending up at the same place, they won't be able to follow each other. The first team to finish the course is declared the winner. This should take about an hour.

Bike Tour:

Last on the activity list is a bike ride to a not-too-distant park or beach for a hamburger or hot-dog feed.

BICYCLE RODEO

Here is another collection of bike games which may be included in an all-day bicycle outing for your youth group:

1. *Calf-roping:* Have one person stand in the center of an open area and each contestant tries to "rope the calf" as he rides by on a bicycle. After a rider successfully "lassoes" the person in the middle, he should immediately drop the rope to avoid injury to himself or the "calf." The calf may duck, but he must keep his hands at his sides and stay on his feet.

2. *Bull-dogging:* This is rough. Have some big guys play the bulls. (Have them use football gear if they have it). The cowboys and bulls line up about 10 feet apart. When the whistle blows, the bull runs straight out. The cowboy goes after him. Cowboy jumps from bike and tries to

bring the bull down. The bull tries to keep going on his feet as long as he can. Use old bikes, as they could possibly be damaged. This game should not be played on pavement or hard ground. Fastest time wins.

3. *The 100-Yard Crawl:* Bikes must travel in a straight line to a finish line 100 yards away. The idea is to go as *slowly* as possible. If a rider touches a foot or any part of his body to the ground (trying to maintain his balance), or goes off course, he is disqualified. The last person to finish wins.

4. *Bike Cross-country:* This is an obstacle race that may include anything you want, the rougher the better. From a starting point, bikes compete for time. On the trail have a "log jump" (4-inch log that the bike must jump over). "Tight rope" (a 2x6, 12 ft. long about 6 inches off the ground). A "Limbo Branch" (low tree branch or board about 10 inches above the handle bars). "Tire Weave" (8 or 10 old tires set up in a row about 6 ft. apart). The one to complete the course in the shortest time wins. You can change penalties for those who mess up on some of the obstacles.

5. *100-Yard Spring:* This is a regular 100-yard dash from a standstill with bikes.

6. *Bike Pack:* See how many can fit on a bike and still go 10 feet.

7. *Bicycle Demolition:* Have all bike riders form a large circle. You will need about 100 feet diameter. They may each have all the water balloons they can carry. (Stuffed in shirts, pockets, etc.). When the whistle blows, they all interweave in the circle and let each other have it!

BIGGER AND BETTER HUNT

The entire group meets at a central location for instructions. Divide the group into teams. Each team selects a captain and is given a penalty to begin with. The idea is for the team to go to someone's home in the neighborhood and trade the penny for something "bigger and better." They then take the item they received in trade for the penny to the next house and attempt to trade that item again for something "bigger and better." The team is not allowed to trade for cash. It has to be an item that the person at each house is willing to give in exchange for whatever the team has at that time. Team members are not allowed to "sweeten the pot" by adding more money to the original penny or any of the items along the way. Each team has one hour (or so), and at the end of the time limit, the teams meet back at the central location and show what they finally ended up with. The group with the "biggest and the best" is the winner. This has been used successfully with many different groups, and some groups have traded for such items as washing machines, watermelons, electric toasters, and all kinds of usable stuff. The items collected can be used later in a rummage sale, or may be donated to a local service organization.

BIKE HIKE

Have an all-day outing on bicycles. Plan a route that encompasses 5 to 10 miles out in the country or wherever traffic is light and good riding trails are available. Take sack lunches and have lunch while on the trip. Have the group wind up at a parking lot or large area where a "Bike Olympics" can then be held. These events are good possibilities:

1. *Baton Relay:* Ride bike across the parking lot and hand off baton to next rider on the team.

2. *Slalom Race:* Contestants are timed as they ride bikes through a slalom course. Have a stop watch on hand.

3. *Snail Race:* Mark off a narrow trail and riders must try to stay in the trail and ride as *slowly* as possible. Feet may not touch the ground. The rider with the longest time wins.

4. *Straw Race:* Place coke bottles all over the parking lot with drinking straws in them. Bike riders must ride up to the bottles and pick up the straws with their bare toes, then reach down with their hands and take from their toes.

BIKE PROGRESSIVE DINNER

A good variation of the old "Progressive Dinner" is to have everyone travel on bicycles. Another is to get tandem bikes and have the guy in the rear feed the guy in front as they travel along.

BIKE RALLY

Although this could be classed as a "special event," it is a great idea for an image builder or promotional event for your youth program. Because of the valuable prizes involved (either donated or purchased), this bike rally attracts a great deal of attention. It would be helpful to prepare rules and regulations as well as a publicity piece on a large bike rally like this:

Rules:

This bicycle rally will be a competition event with a route divided into five time segments or divisions. There will be an allotted amount of time given to complete each segment, with a beginning and ending time given the competitors for each one. In no way is this a race to beat the next person. The competitors will be started at 15 to 30 second intervals. A certain amount of "skill" will be required individually, as each division will be timed and minus points given for early and late arrivals at the beginning and end of each segment, or check point. The following rules and regulations will be the official guidelines:

1. This bike rally will be open to high school students only.

2. Competitors will meet at the _____ parking lot at 1:30 P.M. on _____.

3. Each competitor will receive a "rally number" to be worn throughout the rally. These numbers will be issued between 1:30 and 1:55 P.M. the day of the rally. Latecomers will forfeit their eligibility and entry fee.

4. There will be a one dollar entry fee. Entries must be in by _____ (2 days before). Late entries up to _____ 1:30 P.M. the day of the event will be $1.50.

5. Each competitor will have a starting time, with all of the competitors being started at 15 to 30 second intervals.

6. There will be five sets of directions for the five prospective segments in the route. Directions will be given individu-

ally as the segments are run, with new directions being given for the next leg of the journey.

7. Each competitor must have a Rally Entry Ticket, a watch with second hand, and a man-powered bicycle (no motorized vehicles allowed).

8. Both boys and girls will compete under the same standards as outlined in these Rules and Regulations.

9. An official will be at each traffic sign to insure safe and legal competition and enforce the regulations of traffic signals.

10. The officials timepieces will be synchronized and will be the final determining timepieces.

11. The officials judgments will prevail.

12. The person with the least number of points will win. Points will be given as outlined in the following Rally Regulations.

Regulations:

The following violations will be in effect during this rally:

For each second you are late at a check point — 3 points

Failure to observe traffic regulations, stop signs, turning signals, etc. — 50 points for each violation

Taking an alternate route to reach a check point — 100 points

Helping another competitor — 100 points

Being helped by another competitor — 100 points

"Team riding" to help a certain competitor win — 500 points

Stopping at other than a traffic signal — 10 points

Failure, for any reason, to wear competition number — 1,000 points

Harassing another competitor — 100 points

Messing around; such things as interfering with traffic, weaving around on both sides of the road, etc. (This does not include wheelees.) — 50 points per incident

Such misfortunes as blown tires, broken spokes, etc. will just have to suffer the minus points which could result in late arrivals.

Deviation from the prescribed route for any reason — 500 points

BIKE SIT

Since many people don't like to ride their bikes (only sit on them), this activity is designed to enable even the sitters to have fun. Most areas of the country have an extended downgrade of road. Simply truck all the bikes to the top of this downgrade and let the contestants sit on their bikes all the way to the bottom. Some downgrades last for twenty miles! There can be variations, too: for those select boys who have a lot of energy, let them try to ride up the downgrade; or see who can coast the farthest without pedaling.

BLOW-OUT

A "Blow-out" is a special event based on tires, or cars. Choose up teams, name them ("The Uniroyals," "The Goodyears," etc.), and play some of these wild games:

1. *Tire Relay:* Roll a tire with a person inside it. Race relay style.

2. *Inner Tube Pack:* See how many players each team can get inside a large tractor tire tube (around their waists).

3. *Scavenger Hunt:* Kids go around the neighborhood and try to bring back old tires or inner tubes.

4. *Tire Change:* Teams race to see which can change a tire on all four wheels in the shortest length of time.

5. *Tire Slalom:* Set up a slalom course and teams roll the tires along the course all at the same time. Turning sharp corners is not easy, and players running their tires into each other become a real problem.

6. *Tire Stack:* If you have enough tires, teams compete to see which can stack a pile of tires one on top of the other the highest.

7. *Tire Eat:* This is like a pie eating contest, only you use an "Angel Food Cake" which has a hole in the middle and resembles a tire. Each team chooses one hungry player to compete.

8. *Capture the Tube!* Put all the tires and tubes in the middle, with each team's territory marked off around the tubes. On a signal, the players grab the tires and try to get as many as they can into their territory. Once it is in a team's territory, it cannot be captured by any other team.

BLUE GNU

Obtain five or six people who are strangers to your group. Assign each a name such as: The Blue Gnu, The Pink Panda, The Yellow Yak, The Green Goose, The Purple Parakeet, The Red Rhino, etc. Have each of these people wear an item of clothing that is the same color as the color in their assigned "name" and then go to a shopping center and mix in the crowd of shoppers. Then the kids in your youth group are sent out in pairs to the shopping center to find these animals. They must go up to strangers and, depending on what color they are wearing, ask them questions like, "Are you the Blue Gnu?" If they are right, they get the person's real name and after the players return to the meeting place, the ones who get the most names right win. The couple to get them *all* (first) is the grand prize winner. Set a time limit.

BUG NIGHT

This event is good if you have many people who drive Volkswagens. Get four or five VW "bugs" (sedans) and play some of the following games. Each team gets a Volkswagen.

The cars must be pushed everywhere. This event should be held on a large parking lot or paved surface where there is plenty of room. Here are the games:

1. *Best Dressed Beetle:* Each team should decorate its car as elaborately as possible. This event may be advertised ahead of time, and made a prerequisite for entry of a car in the event, which would result in more elaborate dec-

orating. If not, provide some materials for each team to decorate with.

2. *Bug Race:* Each car needs a driver and power to move. Begin with car in neutral. The players then push the car as fast as they can down a straight track for 100 yards. Use starting gun and a stopwatch. The driver steers and applies brakes at the end of the track. This is done one at a time.

3. *Obstacle Course:* Similar to above race, except a course should be set up slalom style, zig-zagging around various obstacles.

4. *Tire Change:* Teams change a tire on their car without using a jack in the fastest time.

5. *Backward Bug Race:* Same as the Men's Bug Race, only the car is pushed in reverse. Make sure there are no spectators or obstacles along the sides of the track.

6. *Bug Smash:* See if you can obtain an old junk VW body from a car salvage company, and bring it to the Bug Night. Then give one guy from each team a swing with a sledgehammer. Whoever does the most damage wins.

COBBLER GOBBLER

This is a baking contest combined with a scavenger hunt. Divide the group into teams of five, with boys and girls on each team. Each team is given a list of ingredients to find (sugar, flour, fruit, etc.). When the team collects all its ingredients, it reports back to the starting place (or wherever you have the use of large ovens) and a recipe for fruit cobbler is given to the team. All teams get the same recipe, except maybe for a different fruit in each. After the cobbler is prepared, it goes into the oven. (While the cobbler is cooking, table games may be played by the team members.) After all the cobblers are done, have judges taste each one and award points for the best tasting, first finished, neatest job, etc. The team with the best score gets ice cream to eat with its cobbler. Everyone else gets whipped cream.

COME AS YOU WERE PARTY

The theme of this event is babies. Everyone is supposed to come to the party dressed up like a baby. Then try some of these games:

1. *Best Dressed Baby:* Judge for the best costume worn to the party.

2. *Baby Picture Guess:* All the guests bring a baby picture of themselves, and you hang them all up on the wall. Players then try to match them up.

3. *Baby Burp:* Select a couple from each team. The boys drink a bottle of pop and try to burp while the girls slap them on the back. Do it one at a time, and judge for the loudest, longest, etc.

4. *Bottle Drinking Contest:* Give guys a baby bottle full of warm milk. The first to finish it wins.

5. *Diaper Change:* Give girls large diapers (ripped-up sheets) and they race to diaper the guys (over their pants, of course). Or, let the guys race to see who can change a diaper on a doll the fastest.

6. *Baby Food Race:* The girls feed a jar of baby food to the guys. First to finish wins.

7. *Crying Contest:* See who can cry the loudest, most convincingly, etc.

DYE FIGHTS

This is a very successful party or special event that can be a real crowd-puller. Have all your people meet out on a playing field or vacant lot and supply them with either squirt guns or water balloons. The water is mixed with food dye, however, and therefore when you get hit with water you also get colored, as well (you dye!). This may be done a number of ways, but usually a big free-for-all is the most fun. At the end, whoever is the least "dyed" wins. To fill up water balloons, put a little dye in the balloon first, then add water. After the fight, have all the kids meet at a local hamburger stand for food. People who see them can't believe their eyes. A variation of this is to use squirt guns and red dye only. A game of cowboys and Indians is then played in which two teams each try to eliminate the other by hitting them with the red water. When you are hit, you are out of the game. Last guy to get his is the winner for his team.

FIGHT NIGHT

Have kids come in their grubbies, meet in a vacant lot or a big back yard that can be messed up real good. Rope off a square arena (about 20' by 20') and explain that all fighting will be done inside that square. Choose two boys' teams and two girls' teams of from 5 to 10 on a team. Boys fight each other first, then the girls. Spectators judge to determine the winners.

The events are done in rounds. The teams get in their corners (like a boxing match) and the ammo is placed in the center of the arena. When the horn or whistle sounds, they come out of the corners, grab the ammo, and start fighting until the horn blows again, which ends that round.

Round One — *Water balloons*
Round Two — *Tomatoes*
Round Three — *Eggs*
Round Four — *Flour*
Round Five — *Mud*

Make sure no one brings his own ammo. You provide it all. At the end of each round, the contestants go to their corners, and you bring out the eggs, or tomatoes, or whatever and place them in the middle of the arena. Check with your local grocers and there is a good chance that you can get old or spoiled merchandise for this. Mix the mud ahead of time. Dump it in the arena with buckets or a wheelbarrow. The flour would be in little lunch bags, so that everyone on the team gets one. Rounds should be one minute in length.

Players may wear anything they want for protection, such as football helmets, raincoats, etc. Usually they just get in the way. The winner is the cleanest team when it's all over.

Announce that no throwing of the ammo is allowed. The fighters must pick up the eggs, for example, and break them on the other person, not throw them at each other.

Be sure you have plenty of supervision, especially if you have a large number on hand, or many new people. Take Super 8 movies of the action, and show them later to the group. They won't believe they are seeing themselves. After the fights, rinse everyone down with a garden hose to clean them off.

FOOT PARTY

Here's a great party idea to "kick" off your social activities. First of all, divide the group into teams and have them choose a name. (It must have something to do with feet, i.e., toe jams, bunions, etc.) The remainder of the evening is spent in foot competition:

Foot Painting Contest: Teams choose an "artist" to draw pictures with feet. "Best" picture wins.

Foot Awards: Award points and prizes for the largest foot, smallest foot, ugliest foot, funniest foot, smelliest foot, etc.

Foot Footage: Have teams line up their feet toe to heel. The team with longest combined length wins.

Foot Stack: Stack feet on top of each other. Group with the highest stack wins.

FOOT SMASH

This is an evening of fun built around the "foot." The group is divided into teams, and the following games may be played:

1. Each group is given newsprint and paper plates with poster paint, and must paint a mural using their bare feet only on the paper. Best "picture" wins.

2. Each group selects the biggest, smallest, and most unusual (or ugliest) foot in the group and prizes are awarded for the winners in each category. Special "toe-rings" may be made to designate the winning feet.

3. Each team can make up a song about feet and perform it for the whole group.

4. Other "foot games" from this book and others in the

series can be played, such as "Foot Painting," "Foot Signing," "Foot Wrestling," "Marble Fish" and "Lemon Pass."

At the end of the evening, serve hot dogs, and award cans of "Foot Guard" to the winning team.

THE GREAT RACE

Carloads of players (the same number in each car) leave at the same time, with a list of tasks they must perform. The first team to finish the entire list and return wins the race. Create a list based on your local area and the possibilities it provides. A sample list: (May be adapted for your area)

1. Go to the Union Bank Building. Park on the fourth level of their parking lot (if full, wait until a space is available). Everyone go in the bank. One at a time, each member of your team must ride the elevator from the first floor to the twenty-first floor and back down again.

2. Next, go to Central Park. Everyone take the free tour of the science museum, which is every half hour. The tour lasts fifteen minutes. If you just miss it, wait until the next one.

3. Go to Mayor Smith's home at 4352 Birch Street. Everyone sing any Christmas carol you wish, standing on his front porch.

4. Go to Highway 41. Use the trash bag provided and fill it full of litter from along the highway. Do not take cans from any litter cans along the highway and do not pick up rocks, leaves, etc. Only paper, cans, bottles and other trash.

You can make up other tasks, set a time limit, etc. A sponsor should ride with each group to guard against cheating. The group to finish most of the tasks in the time limit wins, or the first to finish them all wins.

GROCERY STORE CAR RALLY

Divide your group into cars. Each car load gets twenty shiny new pennies. Instruct players to buy twenty pieces of bubble gum from twenty different grocery stores and bring back a receipt for each penny spent. Prizes are awarded on the basis of speed and variety. A team may win by doing it in the shortest time or trading in stores that no one else contacted.

GUINNESS GAMES

Here's a great idea that can become an annual event for your youth group. Have a day of contests in which contestants may try to set a "world's record" a la *The Guinness Book of World Records*. However, players do not compete against the Guinness book, but against themselves. The first year, "records" are set and the following year contestants try to break them with new records established which last for another year. Here are a few sample contests:

Eating Contests (amount of food eaten with a given time limit)
1. Hamburgers
2. Tacos
3. Sloppy Joes
4. Marshmallows
5. Lemon wedges
6. Onions
7. Bananas

Endurance Contests (Time)
1. Standing on your head
2. Running in place
3. Talking
4. Stare down
5. Pogo stick jumping
6. Dribbling a basketball
7. Keeping eyes open without blinking

Skill Contests
1. Free throw shooting (percentage of shots)
2. Frisbee throwing (distance)
3. Marshmallow throwing (distance)
4. Burping (number in succession)
5. Bubble blowing (number in succession)
6. Various games (highest score)

Other Contests
1. Volkswagen Stuff (number of players inside)
2. Hula Hoop Pack
3. Marshmallows stuffed in mouth (number)

There can be a separate boys and girls category in the athletic contests. Kids can pay an "entry" fee, and sign up for whichever events they would like to try. "Trophies" can be presented to the new record holders.

HOGWASH

A "Hogwash" is an outdoor event designed around pigs. You will need to acquire a couple of pigs from a nearby farm or school. You will also need to cage them so they won't run off. Then choose up teams and play some of these games:

1. *Name the Pig Contest.* If you have one pig for each team, let each team name its pig. Judge the best name, and give a booby prize to the worst names.

2. *Pickled Pigs Feet Eating Contest.* Get them at a grocery store and have one person from each team race to see who can eat the most the fastest.

3. *Pig Decorating Contest.* Provide shaving cream, hats, ribbons, clothes, and whatever you have on hand, and each team decorates its pig. Set a time limit.

4. *Pig Washing Contest* (A "Hogwash"). Give each team soap, talcum powder, deodorant, etc. and each team tries to make its pig as "lovely" as possible.

5. *Tail Tie.* With all the pigs in the pen, each team has one of its players locate its pig, chase it down, and tie a ribbon on its tail.

6. *Pigpen Contest.* This is the "Pigpen" from the famous "Peanuts" comic strip. The idea is for each team to select one of its members to decorate as ugly and dirty as possible. Use mud, dirt, old rags, charcoal, or whatever.

7. *Hog Calling Contest.* With the pigs a certain distance

away, teams try to call their pig ("Soooo-eeeeeee!") in the fastest time. Pigs should be placed in the middle of the pigpen, with the kids surrounding them. This should be done one team at a time, one pig at a time.

8. *Mud Fight.* Dig a mud hole and have one minute mud fights. The cleanest team is the winner.

9. *Pig Feed.* Serve refreshments (ice cream, etc.) in a trough ("V" shaped, made out of wood, lined with tin foil) and kids eat without using their hands.

HOUSEWIVES MARATHON

Here's a game for all those "women's lib" girls who always feel "oppressed" by being made to play those rough boys' games. It works great when played boys against the girls. The order of events is listed below. Team members randomly have their names placed in the spaces:

1. _____ must run to an oven and fry an egg (to judge's satisfaction) and eat it (pass apron).

2. _____ must kiss good-by to _____, _____, _____, and _____ who represent a husband going off to work (pass apron).

3. _____ must sweep an area clean (we used a tent since we were at camp) (pass apron).

4. _____ must wash and hang up to dry one T shirt, supplied by that team (pass apron).

5. _____ must eat a low calorie lunch (we used prune-flavored yogurt) (pass apron).

6. _____ must roll his/her hair with two curlers (pass apron).

7. _____ must sew one button on a shirt passing the thread through each hole in the button at least three times (pass apron).

8. _____ must set a table for two, since the children are eating at a friends this evening (pass apron).

9. _____ must freshen up by using lipstick, eye-liner, perfume and nose powder (pass apron).

10. _____ must open a can (we used sauerkraut) with an old-fashioned can opener, and _____ must eat it and belch.

INNER TUBE OLYMPICS

This is a good snow sport (obviously usable only during the winter months). All you need is a steep slope covered with snow, and inner tubes. Either make competition individual or by teams. You (the leader) are the only judge and commentator. The events are: Men and Women's Singles, Men and Women's Doubles, Mixed Doubles, Stunt Riding, Slalom, etc. You award points for *distance*, *ride* and *form*. Poor form criteria: wiping-out, turning the innertube while riding it down the hill, closing eyes, etc. Stunt riding is based on originality and ingenuity.

MILK CARTON BOAT RACE

Each of two (or more) teams is given four rolls of heating duct tape and instructed to build a boat using only milk cartons and tape. Points should be given for:

1. Number of cartons used.

2. Originality.

3. Number of pounds of weight boat will support in water without sinking or capsizing.

4. Winner of race (200-300 yards).

Excitement should be built up during the week until the judging and race on the last day of camp.

MISSING PERSONS PARTY

This event may be held on foot or using cars. It takes place in a shopping center or business district on a late shopping night when the stores are open. Select 10 to 20 players to be "missing" in the shopping area. Take pictures of the "victims" in normal dress. These are given to the groups looking for them.

The people who are going to be missing meet together ahead of time and make up riddles or clues as to where they will be. They also select a disguise appropriate to themselves and their surroundings. For example, players may disguise themselves as bus drivers, cab drivers, old men, blind men, nuns, pregnant young wives, a man in a wheelchair, repairmen, store clerk, or anything that they think they can "pull off."

The rest of the group are the "manhunters." They meet at some central location in the shopping area and divide up into groups of from 6 to 10 per group. Each group gets pictures of the victims and the set of riddles and clues in numerical order. Each group is to stick together for the duration of the hunt. When a hunter thinks he has spotted a victim, he approaches the suspected person and says some sort of password like "Beep Beep!" If the person is a victim, then he must admit he has been found. He then tells whether or not there is another missing person with him. If there is another, the hunter informs his group and they continue the hunt. If not, the group goes on after the next victim. The first group to find all its "missing people" wins.

This game works best when you can go in with another youth group and have one group be the "victims" and one group be the "hunters." That way, the players don't know each other very well, which means they will be more difficult to find. Also, it gives you more people to participate in the hunt, which makes it more fun. If you have, say, 30 missing people and 30 hunters, then give each hunting group (of 6 per group) 6 missing people to find. Each group hunts for a different bunch of victims. That way you only need one picture of each victim, rather than several (one for each hunting group). Preparation is an obvious requirement of this game. Pictures and disguises must be arranged for ahead of time.

You can add another twist to this game by having the hunters "kill" the victims rather than just find them. At the same time, the victims can "kill" the hunters. The killing is done by getting a sticker or piece of tape off the back of the other person. If the victims can kill off more than half the hunting group, then the group has to call off its hunt and is out of the game. However, the hunters have the advantage, so they must "kill" all their victims.

This basic idea may be changed or adapted to meet your own local requirements. It can be called a "Manhunt" or any other name you choose.

MISSION IMPOSSIBLE

Divide the entire group into cars or buses (depending on the size of your crowd). Each group has a leader, who goes with them to make sure they don't cheat on the rules of the game: (1) Each team gets a list of "Impossible Missions" which they must accomplish within the given time limit. (2) They must take each mission in the order in which it appears on the list. (Each list has the same missions, but arranged differently, so that everyone doesn't go on the same exact route.) (3) They cannot tell anyone they come in contact with *why* they are going about their mission until that mission has been accomplished. (In other words, they can't go up to someone and say, "Will you help us? We are playing a game, and we need. . . .") The team which completes its list of missions and returns to the starting area first, wins.

Some sample Impossible Missions:

1. Convince another person (off the street, or a stranger) to come with you to help accomplish the other missions.

2. Entire group must do an Indian rain dance around the fountain at the courthouse square.

3. Get a signed statement from a doctor saying you do not have the bubonic plague.

4. Everybody hop around the block surrounding the city park on one foot.

5. Find an on-duty policeman and report a U.F.O.

6. Find a tennis court where people are playing and each of you take a turn at hitting the ball over the net.

7. Go to a college girls dormitory and serenade the girls with "We wish you a Merry Christmas."

8. Talk a taxicab driver into driving the entire group around the block for only a dollar.

NEWSPAPER RALLY

The following is a good special event, centered around newspapers. To prepare for it, get a huge pile of old newspapers, the more the better. The following list of games may be played with two or more teams.

1. *Newspaper Costume Race:* Teams have five minutes (or so) to dress players up with newspaper to look like certain things. For example, Santa and his reindeer, Butch Cassidy and the Sundance Kid, Snow White and the Seven Dwarfs, etc. Tape may be provided each team to help them construct the costumes. Judge for the best job.

2. *Newspaper Treasure Hunt:* Put in each team's pile of papers an equal number of specially colored pages. The team to find the most of them in the time limit wins.

3. *Newspaper Scavenger Hunt:* Call out certain items from the papers and the first team to find them wins. For example, a Honda ad, a want-ad for a 1956 Chevy, a news item about a murder, etc.

4. *Wad and Pile:* Teams get ten minutes to wad up all their paper into a big pile. The highest pile wins.

5. *Hide and Seek:* Hide as many players as possible under the pile of wadded-up papers. The team with the most players out of sight wins. Set a time limit.

6. *Compact Newspapers:* Teams try to compact the paper on their side into the smallest pile possible.

7. *Snow Fight:* Make a line of chairs between the two teams. On a signal, the teams throw all their paper on the other team's side. When time is up (2 or 3 minutes), the team with the least amount of paper on their side wins.

8. *Disposal Event:* Give each team plastic trash bags. The team to get all of the paper in the bags in the shortest time wins.

OLD-FASHIONED WATER FIGHT

Divide your group into two teams. Each team has a big barrel they must fill with water. There should be hoses, water balloons, buckets, etc. available. The object is to fill your barrel and prevent the filling by other teams. The barrels are filled by wringing out clothes, stealing other team's water, capturing hoses, etc.

PEANUTS PICNIC

This special event is based on the immortal "Peanuts" comic strip characters, created by Charles Schulz, and is a great fun activity for junior highs. Advertise it as a "Peanuts Picnic," using posters, passouts, etc. incorporating the Peanuts characters as much as possible. Refreshments can include peanuts, peanut butter sandwiches, etc. Play the games below, plus any others you can think of that might fit the various characters, and award appropriate prizes to the winning teams. (Many stores carry a wide variety of "Peanuts" toys and gifts.)

1. *"Charlie Brown's Game":* This is a game of modified softball. Play the game on a normal softball diamond, only use a "mushball," and run the bases in reverse order. The infield cannot throw the ball, but they can pick it up and run with it to tag the runner or the bases. Three innings are played, with two outs per inning. The points scored are given to the other team, and the team with the most points loses. All other rules are the same as regular softball.

2. *"Linus' Game":* This one may also be called "Steal the Security Blanket." A blanket is placed in the center of a large square, and each team lines up on one side of the square (there should be four teams). Each team should number off 1-2-3-4-etc., so that each player has a number. To begin the game, one (or more) numbers are called out by the leader, and all the players on each team with the corresponding number(s) run to the center and try to pull the blanket across their team's side of the square. As soon as any part of the blanket crosses their

side, a point is scored and the blanket is returned to the center of the square and the players return to their sides. A new number or numbers is called and the game is over as soon as everyone is sick and tired of playing it. For best results, use a "blanket" made of very tough material, like canvas.

3. *"Snoopy's Game":* This is a "doghouse pack," which requires the acquisition of or the building of a "doghouse." Each team simply tries to see how many people they can pack inside and on top of the doghouse within a given time limit. The team that gets the most people in and on it is the winner.

4. *"Red Baron vs. Snoopy Game":* This game should be played on a large open field, or in an open wooded area. Draw a line of demarcation which separates the Red Baron's territory from Snoopy's territory. The group is divided in half, with all the "Red Barons" in their territory and all the "Snoopys" in their territory. Each player on the Snoopy team has a "tail," which can be a flag (like those used in flag football) or a piece of tape on their clothing. Before the game begins, the Snoopys gather at the end of their territory, as far away from the line of demarcation as possible, and the Red Barons line up on the line. On a signal, the Snoopy players try to get into Red Baron territory with their tails still on, and the Red Baron players try to capture tails before they cross the line. The Snoopy team gets a point for every tail they get into Red Baron territory, and the Red Baron team gets a point for each tail they capture.

5. *"Schroeder's Game":* Shroeder is the little boy who loves to play his little toy piano, and this game is a musical one. Each team must compose and perform a short team "song." A panel of judges selects the winner.

6. *"Pig Pen's Game":* Each team decorates one member of their team to look like the "Pig Pen" character. Mud, grease, dirt, charcoal, marking pens, torn clothes, etc.,

may be used to make the person look as dirty as possible. A panel of judges may select the winner.

SHOPPING CENTER GAME

Take the players to a local shopping center or downtown area where there are plenty of stores within walking distance. Then divide into small groups and give each group a list similar to the one below. The kids are to fill in the blanks by "comparison shopping," that is — trying to find the best bargains available. The groups with the most blanks filled in and the best prices (within the time limit) wins. Think up twenty or thirty questions such as these:

1. The cheapest pair of size 12 snow boots.
   Store _____   Price_____

2. An "afro" wig.
   Store _____   Price _____

3. One pair of size 16 boys shorts.
   Store _____   Price _____

4. The best laxative available (recommended by a druggist).
   Store _____ Brand _____ Price _____

5. A "head gasket."
   Store _____   Price _____

6. Twenty-five wedding invitations.
   Store_____   Price _____

7. A heart-shaped locket.
   Store _____   Price _____

8. Five pound sack of "Puppy Chow."
   Store_____   Price _____

9. Ten party balloons.
   Store _____   Price _____

SNOW SCULPTING

This game is great for winter camps and whenever snow is on the ground. Divide the group into teams, and have each group find a spot where the snow is good and thick. They must "sculpture" anything they want within a given time limit. Encourage them to be as creative as possible. Traditional "snowmen" are not allowed. Sample "sculptures" might include: Cars, famous personalities, buildings, cartoon characters, animals, Santa and his reindeer, etc. Judge to determine the most creative, best job, and degree of difficulty.

SNOWSHOE OLYMPICS

If you live in an area where winters are white, you might try this. Take kids on a hike in the mountains on snowshoes. Then try races, obstacle course runs, and even a game of soccer on snowshoes. The results can be a lot of fun.

TOWN STAMPING

This is a great special event to be carried out in cars or on bikes. Teams of 5-10 members each are chosen, and each team selects a team captain. On a signal, the teams leave the meeting place in cars or on bikes, and at each intersection, the team captain flips two coins to determine which direction they will go:

1. *If both coins are heads, the team goes right.*

2. *If both are tails, the team goes left.*

3. *If one is heads and the other is tails, the team goes straight ahead.*

At the end of 10 flips of the coins (ten intersections), the team to get the farthest away from the original location is the winner. Or, you may set a time limit, and the team to get the farthest away at the end of the time limit (regardless of how many times they have to flip their coins) is the winner.

TREASURE HUNTS

The "Treasure Hunt" has been an old stand-by for many years, but it has rarely been done well. The following is a guide to enable you to inject new life into this old idea, and make it an exciting experience every time you use it. (Yes, you *can* use it more than once!)

The first thing to remember is that to create interest you must make it a new event. For example, rather than calling it a Treasure Hunt, make the treasure a live goose hidden somewhere, and call it a "Wild Goose Chase." Or the object of the hunt might be a snowman built somewhere in town, and you can then have a "Search for the Abominable Snowman." One group obtained a live hippopotamus and had a "Hippo Hunt." All the players wore safari hats and followed the clues to the hippo which was tied up in the middle of the city's largest shopping center. This is where your own creativity becomes important. The possibilities are endless. Just don't rely on the same old thing over and over again.

In case you are not familiar with the basics of a treasure hunt, the idea is for participants to locate the "treasure," and be the first to do so. This is done by solving a number of "clues" placed in different locations, with each clue leading to another clue and then finally to the "treasure" itself.

The Hunt Begins:

Have everyone meet at a certain time and place and assign them all to cars or buses (depending on the size of the crowd). Have each vehicle appoint a leader or captain and then have a brief meeting with each of the captains to explain the rules and begin the hunt. The rules should include the following:

1. Time Limit. At a certain time the hunt is over regardless of whether or not the treasure has been found. Two hours is plenty of time for most hunts.

2. Explanation of the "Clue Packet."

3. The first clue is given to the captains at this time. The clue is sealed in an envelope, and when you give the signal (whistle or racing flag, etc.) the clues are opened and the hunt is off and running. Each captain opens the clues, takes it to his team and as soon as they figure out the clue, they go where the clue takes them.

The Clues:

Each vehicle should be numbered, and in your planning of the hunt, you should plan for each vehicle to take a different route to the treasure. That prevents the groups from simply following each other. Each vehicle should go to all the same places, just in a different order.

Each clue will take the vehicle to one of six locations (more or less if you want). The last location is where the treasure is. The winner must decipher all the clues as well as locate the treasure. If you somehow are able to cheat and locate the treasure without working out all the clues, you are penalized. Each clue leads to the next clue, and you must take them in order.

The leader giving out the clues does not participate in the hunt itself. The clues are numbered so that each group gets the right clue to keep them on the right course. Sometimes it adds to the fun to have the "Clue Giver" hidden at the clue location, and the kids have to find him in some way. For example, if the location is a restaurant, the "Clue Giver" might be sitting at a table eating. The kids must find him by saying the "secret word" to everyone in the place, until they get the right response (and the clue) from the right person. Of course, if you do this, you need to use someone the players won't recognize. Also, be sure to get permission to do this from the owners of the restaurant, store, etc.

Make the clues difficult. Unless the players are very young, they can usually figure out a lot more than we think. The clues may take many forms, such as these samples actually used in a treasure hunt in San Diego, California:

1. An envelope containing an egg yolk and a piece of ham. (Yolk plus ham equals "yokahama," or a landmark in San Diego called the "Yokahama Bell.")

2. A piece of paper with the letters "IIDEORPS," which, when unscrambled, spell out a park in San Diego called "Presidio" Park.

3. A list of numbers:
   23456
   26576
   67934
   94376
   etc.

When the numbers are added up, they give a phone number, and the group is to go to a phone booth and use the coins in the "clue packet" to call the number and find the next location.

4. A set of instructions for the team captains:

    a. Divide the entire crowd into four small groups and give each small group one of these sounds:

        LLL
        DUH
        SEE
        WHR

    b. Have the groups combine sounds until they make sense. (Sea World)

Clue Packets:

Each group is given a manila envelope full of things that may or may not be important to them. They get the packet at the beginning of the hunt and the captains are instructed to familiarize themselves with its contents immediately.

1. A sheet with numbers and arrows pointing to certain locations. *Only* the locations marked are possible clue locations. They may not be a clue location, but only the marked ones are possibilities.

2. *Rules* (basic instructions).

3. *General Clue sheet.* This sheet contains clue phrases that may or may not be important to the clues. If a group is having a difficult time with a certain clue they should check the general clue sheet to see if it will help. Example phrases might be:

    a. The first two letters are all you need.
    b. Shamu lives there.
    c. Blue is a pretty color.

4. *General clue items.* General clue items are odds and ends that may or may not be of help in solving some or all the

clues. Items could be punched IBM cards, a dime, band-aid, etc.

5. *Emergency Clues.* If a group is unable to figure out their clue, then they can open an emergency clue, which is very easy, and continue the hunt. However, each vehicle is penalized 15 minutes for each emergency clue used. The emergency clues are numbered and sealed in envelopes just like the regular clues and they must be turned in at the treasure location. If any are opened, then they must wait out their penalty time before they can claim the treasure. If another group should arrive during that penalty time with no emergency clues opened, they would win.

Some Reminders:

If the treasure is not found, the winner is determined by who got the farthest using the least amount of emergency clues. This really should not happen, though. Plan enough time so that everyone will get to the treasure.

If the treasure itself is not something the players can keep, then have some appropriate prizes to give to the winning group. Have a presentation of the hunt "trophy" to the team captain and make a big deal out of this.

Don't use the same kind of clue each time. Make them all different, and a new challenge with each clue. This adds tremendously to a good hunt.

Clue locations should be as unusual as possible, such as the top of a church tower, a boat in the middle of a lake, up in a tree, buried in a cemetery, at a tourist attraction, etc.

Make sure speed and traffic laws are obeyed. The drivers should be carefully screened to avoid problems in this area. Make sure drivers have necessary permissions from parents (if they are young people), insurance, and a driver's license. One group put a sponsor in each vehicle who held a spoon with an egg (raw) in it out the window. If the vehicle went too fast, bounced, swerved etc., the egg would drop and break. Penalties were given for each egg broken during the hunt.

It is usually a good idea to have the last place (the location of the treasure) somewhere suitable for a meeting. After all the players are back from the hunt, they can share experiences, you may award prizes, perhaps have some singing, crowd breakers, or a speaker, and some refreshments.

TRICYCLE DERBY

This is a highly successful event to be held in a parking lot, or on any good flat, paved open space. Obtain a number of tricycles, some chalk to mark off the race course and some flags: a green one for "go," a yellow one for "caution," and a checkered one for the "winner." The parking lot is marked off for three separate events (races):

1. *Oval Lap Track* — Run an "Indy 500" type race with two or three laps (500 *yards*, maybe?).

2. *Drag Strip* — Race for fastest time, clocking each driver separately.

3. *Endurance Course* — A race over rocks, around markers and over a pile of dirt, etc. This race is run with one person (girl) sitting on the tricycle with her legs over the handle bars and a second person (boy) pushing from behind with one foot on the back of the tricycle and holding the handle bars, pushing.

Award ribbons and prizes for each event. A winners "wreath" would be a good idea for the grand prize winner.

This activity is best with senior high school players as opposed to junior high. It is more ridiculous for older players and results in a good fun event.

TRICYCLE INTERVIEW

Bring a volunteer to the front of the group and give him two pencils (or two short sticks). Have him sit in a chair facing the group. Tell him that it is very difficult for a person to balance one stick across the point of the other while keeping the legs and feet moving up and down in a rythmic (one-two-three) fashion and to answer questions at the same time. Ask him if he would be willing to give it a try. (Offer a prize if he can do it successfully.) Have him hold the two pencils in a "V" manner, with the ends touching or balancing on each other, and then have him pump his feet up and down. After he does this, begin asking him some questions, like "How much do you weigh?" "What kind of deodorant do you use?" and so on. Finally ask him if he embarrasses easily. He will probably answer, "No." Then ask him if he would be embarrassed to tell the group where he learned to ride his tricycle so well.

TUBING PARTY

This is a great way to spend the afternoon. Find a river or creek deep enough to float down. (Three feet of water is enough to float in.) Then get the word out to your group. Have each person bring an inner tube (sponsors will need to have two or three extras on hand) and some money (at least $ .50). Have transportation arranged to take the contestants and sponsors up the river and let them float back down. A five-mile trip will take most of the afternoon. While the group is floating be sure to stop occasionally to keep the contestants from getting too strung out. Also a sponsor should be in the lead *and* another one bring up the rear of the floating procession. Pre-arrange a spot to get out and have cars there to pick up the group. While the players and sponsors are floating down the river, other sponsors should buy food (with the $ .50) and have it ready when the group gets back. It's tiring, but a lot of fun.

WHAT THE FAT

Here's an idea for a social or party. Give a prize to the person (or group) who comes to the event weighing the most. They can come dressed with rocks and things in their pockets, but must wear what they have on *throughout* the event. Each person is weighed in and (in case of teams) totaled.

WHEELBARROW OLYMPICS

Divide all the players into equal teams of 8 to 10 persons. Each team should have a wheelbarrow. Try to obtain wheelbarrows equally matched in size and weight, and well-built. This event should be held on a grassy field for best results. The following "wheelbarrow games" may then be played:

1. *Wheelbarrow Relay:* Teams line up and team members

pair off. One person rides in the wheelbarrow, and the other pushes. On the starting signal, the wheelbarrow and rider are pushed to a marker about 25 feet away, and the 2 players trade places: the rider becomes the pusher, and vice-versa. Then the next two team members do the same thing, and so on. The first team to finish is the winner. If the wheelbarrow tips over, they must start over. If the teams are small, do it this way: players one and two race up and back, then player three gets into the wheelbarrow, and is pushed up and back by player two. Then player three gets out and becomes the pusher, and player four gets in and rides, and so on.

2. *Wheelbarrow Tube Race:* This is a relay, similar to the preceding one, except that at the marker there is an inner tube, and the players must squeeze through the tube together before returning to the team.

3. *Three-man Relay:* Three members of each team compete at a time with the wheelbarrow. One person rides, and the other two push, with one person on each handle. For added fun, the rider must stand in the wheelbarrow (no squatting or touching the wheelbarrow with his hands).

4. *Hand Wheelbarrow:* This is the old "wheelbarrow race" minus a wheelbarrow. Two players at a time from each team compete in this one. One lies down on the ground, face down, in a push-up position, and the other person holds his feet like a wheelbarrow while the first person walks on his hands. Each pair races to a point and back.

5. *Wheelbarrow Hop:* This is another relay with two members from each team competing at a time. Place the wheelbarrow at the starting line, with the handles facing forward (away from the team). The first pair stands on each side of the wheelbarrow, facing the same direction as the wheelbarrow. On a signal, they place their legs closest to the wheelbarrow into it in a kneeling position. They then grasp the handles in front of them, and hop to the marker and back. Penalties are given if anything but the wheel (or the player's feet) touch the ground.

WITCH HUNT

This is a variation of the old "Treasure Hunt" idea. The "Witch Hunt" is very good for a Halloween special event. The witch is a dummy dressed up like a witch, hidden somewhere in town. Players are divided into teams, each team traveling together, either in a car or a bus. Each team starts out with a clue, and the clues lead the team to further clues and then finally to the witch. All the clues should be written to give a "witchy" feel, such as "With this clue, you'll get your start. Look for a 'stake' to drive through her heart." This clue might send the players to a local steak house, etc. depending on how you set it up. Don't make the clues too easy. After a team finds the witch, they must bring it back to your meeting place to win, so put the witch where it's hard to get. Up in a tree, under a house, in the middle of a shopping center, are all good locations. When the witch is brought in, burn it at the stake, show some horror movies, or have a halloween party.

WRECK IN THE STREET

First of all, get permission from the local police department to block a side street near your location. They will usually be glad to supply barricades. Begin the activities with typical street games such as wheelbarrow races, tricycle races, sack races, ice slide (one sits on block of ice while next man pushes), etc. After about an hour, take a coke break. During this time the players will make needed supplies. Then everyone gathers for the wreck in the street battles; Water balloons, shaving cream, water paint and eggs. Usually the fire department will be glad to wash the streets for you (if not — good luck!). The youth group will talk about this for a long time (the neighbors will too!). It can become an annual event.

WIDE GAMES

WIDE GAMES

CREATE YOUR OWN CAMP GAMES

Old games, such as "Gold Rush," "Capture the Flag," can be adapted to new situations. You can create your own games to fit your own needs, or camp location, or time of year, or whatever, by using the following guidelines:

1. Plan a game with several other people — evaluate every part of it together to see if it will really work, really be fun, really be safe. Two or three of you thinking it out together will soon see loopholes in the game — things that need to be clarified, etc. Try to anticipate ways of cheating and cover them with rules. However, be sure not to stamp out all "creativity" with rules.

2. Ask yourself, "Will everyone be able to play in this game till the end? Is it possible the game could be over in a very short time?" Try to make sure the game is challenging enough to last some time but simple enough so that people will actually feel they are getting somewhere. For example, in the Gold Rush, make sure some gold can be found easily. On the other hand, some of it should be pretty well hidden.

Also be very careful to see that people are "re-cycled." For example, when someone loses his life or is imprisoned, there must be a fairly simple way for him to get back into the game again; otherwise, the game will be very boring for him.

3. Make sure all boundaries are clear. A person must know

when he's safe and when he's not. If the boundaries are really clear, disputes will be kept to a minimum. Make use of clear roads and trails, use string or toilet paper or fires to make clear lines. Also, a number of supervisors on hand at all major spots of conflict can help to quickly rule on disputes before they get out of hand. Keep the game moving!

4. Try to design your games so there is a role for the quieter, non-athletic campers. The Gold Rush is good because defenders only have to shoot water guns. Anyone can look for gold in the bush! Adjust your game to your crowd.

5. Make your scores high. Instead of one point for a prisoner, make it 1,000 or 10,000 etc. It sounds much more impressive.

6. Make sure teams are clearly identifiable — everyone must be able to tell who is on which team (unless the game specifically involves not knowing). Players will tend to try to hide their arm bands or their tape. Stop that one quickly.

7. Watch for safety hazards. Check out areas to be used before each game. Get rid of barbed wire, open wells, dangerous holes, etc. Clearly mark dangerous areas and remind campers of them. Night games in the brush are dangerous. Emphasize "skulking" at night rather than running.

8. The game is to be played by the rules set down. Most of these games will never work unless campers understand the concept of honor. If you are shot — you're dead. If you're clubbed, you must go as a prisoner; if you have been caught, you must give up your gold. Heavily penalize teams that cheat.

9. Make sure leaders understand the game clearly. Always have a few counselors helping the campers on each team. Go over the game rules thoroughly with everyone ahead of time. Use a map to clearly illustrate boundaries. Have leaders in control of the areas where points are made or lost.

10. It is helpful to get the whole camp excited about the game ahead of time, by having some kind of confrontation

between the teams before the game — even just a put-on light or verbal attack between the leaders will help to polarize feeling in the camp and enable people to "feel" the game much more quickly.

ASSASSINATION

The leader and his assistant divide the group into two teams. Each team is to represent a country. In each country, the leader explains, all will be loyal citizens — except one, who will secretly be a spy for the opposing, enemy country.

The leader then gives the following directions; each country's members will move into separate rooms, where they cannot be heard by the enemy country. There they must choose from among their own members a king, who will be unknown by the enemies. After choosing, a spy will be chosen from among the other members of each country by secret drawing of cards, so that the members will not know which one among them is the spy against them. (This is accomplished by the leader having all members of one country except the king draw slips of paper from, say, a bowl, look at his or her slip, and then giving the slip to the leader so he too can see it. All the slips except one will have written on them, "*Loyal.*" The one slip will read, "*Spy.*" Thus the one person alone knows he or she is the spy; the leader will know when the person returns the slip. The assistant does the same with the other country.)

While the countries are still separated, the leader and assistant switch rooms, informing each country the name of their spy on the other team, but not telling them the name of the other country's king.

After this the two countries are brought into the same room. The object is for one country to find out from their spy on the other team who that country's king is, and to assassinate him.

Assassination is done by "stabbing" the enemy with one's finger, in his or her back only!

Each team knows who on the other team is their spy, but they do not know which of their own members is really an enemy spy for the other team. If they can find out, they can assassinate this spy. If they are mistaken and really assassinate one of their loyal members, then they lose the game. Also, if they assassinate one of the members of the other team who is not that country's king, they lose the game.

The spies may use any method they wish to tell their friends on the other team who the king is in the country in which they are spies. But the spies should be subtle, lest they give away their identity to their country's members and be assassinated. Likewise, the country members should be careful not to give away to the other team who is the spy among them, lest they assassinate him.

The country to successfully assassinate the other country's king first, without assassinating anyone by mistake, is the winner.

CHAOS-VS-CONTROL

This is an outdoor spy game best played at a camp where there is plenty of room and good hiding places. It should be played at night and preferably in terrain with many trees, high grass, and the like. Divide into two teams: the "Chaos" agents and the "Control" agents. (You can name the teams anything. The names are not important to the game.) The Chaos agents try to leave the U.S. by reaching a landing strip where their planes are to pick them up. The Control agents try to capture or eliminate the Chaos agents by hitting them with a stocking full of flour. The setup should look like this:

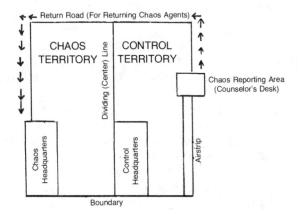

The Chaos agents are safe when in their own territory. They simply have to sneak through Control territory to get to the "airstrip" located behind Control territory. If they manage to get through, they report to a counselor sitting at a desk on the airstrip. They are safe once they get to the airstrip. When they arrive there, they turn over to the counselor a set of "secret plans" (an envelope marked "SST" or "APOLLO," etc.). The Chaos team gets 1000 points for each envelope delivered to the airstrip counselor. Chaos agents may then return to their own headquarters via a path around Control territory to get a new set of plans and try to sneak through again. Control agents may patrol that path to make sure Chaos people are only going back and not coming to the airstrip.

Control agents can only be in their own territory and they must try to spot and club a Chaos agent with their nylon (or newspaper, water balloon, paper bag full of mud, or whatever). If they hit a Chaos agent, the Control agent takes his prisoner to Control headquarters and the Chaos agent must give up his plans. The Control team gets free to try again. Adult counselors should keep score, hand out the plans, etc.

You can use several large flashlights (controlled by counselors) to sweep the entire area to give a "searchlight" effect to the game. The two teams should wear different colored armbands to distinguish them.

DIAMOND SMUGGLING

This indoor camp game was developed for several reasons: (a) Often weather can ruin an outdoor game so that people get wet, muddy or cold. (b) Most camps have plenty of outdoor activities, so less tiring indoor games may be more appropriate. (c) Indoor games do not emphasize athletic ability — rather intelligence and sneakiness. Thus quieter people generally like them better. These games are very good, also, for adults. (d) You can control your campers at night far better with an indoor wide game than an outdoor one. There is virtually no safety hazard and you know where everyone is.

"Diamond Smuggling" is a basic indoor camp game. You will need a fairly large building for this game — a large lounge or dining hall with at least two rooms going off the main room. A school gym will also work.

The Dining Hall is set up as a coffee shop in Paris — one of the rooms off this hall will be the Police Station and another room (preferably not using the same hallway) would be South Africa (The Smugglers Den).

The campers are divided into two teams, the Diamond Smugglers and the Police. The Smugglers divide into two groups, the diamond runners and the diamond smugglers, when they meet privately before the game in the den.

The object is for the whole smuggling team to circulate from their room (named South Africa) into the Coffee Shop (Paris) and back. The runners, whose names are on paper and are about 1/3 of the team, are allowed by the leader to take a diamond (marble) out of South Africa into Paris where they must pass it to a smuggler, who then brings it back to the den and gives it to another adult. The team collects 5,000 points per diamond brought back to the den by a smuggler (not a runner). Runners may not bring a diamond back from Paris. That's why their names need to be written down so those in charge know the difference between runners and smugglers. The police never know the difference because they are never told, otherwise they could seize all runners coming in the door at Paris. All the smugglers and runners need to keep circulating back and forth from South Africa to Paris so the police never know who are runners and who are smugglers.

Paris (the main room) is set up like a coffee shop with lights low — some kind of music and food and drinks being served. Some kids may play games, etc. (a typical restaurant — coffee shop atmosphere). The Paris Police are everywhere in the room (and only in this room). They can arrest anyone they wish on suspicion of possession of stolen diamonds. To arrest someone a policeman simply places his hand on the shoulder of the person he wishes to arrest and says, "You're under arrest." The person must go with the officer to the police station — in no way can he resist arrest or try to ditch a diamond after being arrested. The police officer must accompany his prisoner to the Cop Shop. He presents the person at the door and a counselor takes the arrested man inside. The policeman is then free to go.

The Cop Shop should be a secret place into which the Police can't see. Here counselors confront the arrested person and he must say whether or not he has a diamond. If he does he must give it up and the police get 10,000 points for seizure of the diamond and it's kept there. If the man does not have a diamond the police lose 4,000 for falsely arresting the man. In either case the arrested man is free to go out (preferably by another door) back into circulation in Paris.

This means that if a person is guilty he wants to look innocent; if innocent, he wants to look guilty.

The runners may pass diamonds any way they can devise — in glasses, under the table, in shoes, etc. They may drop a diamond off and let a smuggler know where it is. If a policeman can convince a runner he's a smuggler and get him to give him a diamond, he will simply turn the diamond in at the Cop Shop and the police get 10,000 points. If a policeman finds a diamond he does the same thing.

It is best to run the game 30-40 minutes and then have a half-time in which the teams change roles because the police have a tougher job than the smugglers. Then run the game for another 30-40 minutes. Use about 40 diamonds for a game, involving about 40 people on each team.

FAMILY GAME

This game is great for camps, retreats and special events and is best with a larger group (say 80 or so kids) in an indoor setting, such as a gymnasium or recreation hall.

Divide the group into "families" (8 families of 10, for example). Each family should represent a family immigrating to this country from another. In honor of their immigration to their new home, this game may begin with a banquet (sponsored by the Immigration Department), in which all the families are invited. Each family selects a mother and father and the rest of the children have to have some resemblance to the mother and father, i.e., all exceptionally fat, freckles, hats alike, or something. Each family must also prepare a native dance or native song from their home country to perform at the banquet and also they must introduce their family by their full names to everyone else. The banquet may feature a variety of international dishes to make everyone feel at home.

At the conclusion of the banquet, the "Minister of Immigration" gives a little speech and presents each family with $2,000.00 in cash (play money made up of packets of $50, $100, $500 and $1,000 denominations) and gives "jobs" to about 6 members of each family. A "job" may be an old computer card. It will have a particular occupation written down on it with the salary stated at the bottom. For example, a card might say "This certifies that you are a qualified PLUMBER, Salary: $8,000 per year." Each family is told by the Minister of Immigration that the Government would keep close watch on them and that only those families who really succeeded in their jobs would be allowed to remain in the country. After the banquet is cleared away the game begins.

In the course of the game, 15 minutes represents a year. At the end of each year, the families meet together in a specified place to discuss what happened. At the beginning of each year (indicated by a whistle or bell) each member of the family with a job goes to an area of the room marked with his appropriate job description. For instance, there should be a medical center (for doctors), a trade center, a funeral home, etc. Also, at the beginning of each year, the father goes to the government desk and picks up his family's list of "problems" (see sample "problem card" below), which must be solved in that year. At this time he also gives the government a list of which members of his family have what jobs. In the first year, the problems are not many, but as the years go by, the problems get heavier and heavier. The list might contain from 5 to 12 problems per family that the father has to solve. For example, his house might have plumbing problems — he might need to build a new bathroom. He might have a leaky roof, need new furniture, or need the services of a doctor. There may be deaths in the family; grandmothers, uncles, aunts, children and a funeral director would have to be consulted, along with a minister, perhaps a doctor, hospital, lawyer about the will, etc.

"Problem Cards" may look like this:

Year One
Obtain a place to live
Get a job

Obtain for personal use
form of transportation

Year Two

Pay rent if you do not own a house.	Buy color TV — see furniture store electrician
Succeed at job.	Girlfriend gets sick —
Wheels need balancing — see mechanic	See florist mother bank

For every problem listed, there must be an appropriate "job" to solve the problem. Thus the father may either assign someone else or go himself to the various job areas and have the problem solved by a person who is qualified to do so. To get a problem solved you have to have a qualified plumber, for instance, sign that all the plumbing work has been done in your house and he may charge you according to how difficult the problem seems to be to him. The father then "pays" for the plumber to sign and the signature is put on the problem and at the end of each "year," the Government examines the problem list of each father to see that everything has been taken care of and only people who have a certain job have signed for the work done. If everything is in order, he is given the next year's list; if he does not have everything done, he may be fined several thousand dollars, maybe even up to $10,000 or $20,000 because of the seriousness of not getting certain things done. Then he may be given next year's list and he must go and solve the new problems.

There may also be a Government Employment Center where new jobs are for sale and occasionally it can be announced that there is severe unemployment and everyone has to turn in several jobs. This keeps the job market floating around, thus making it possible for families to improve their position — or to get wiped out, as the case may be. The Employment Center also sells B.A.'s, M.A.'s and Ph.D.'s for fairly high sums. If you are a plumber and have a B.A., you would get 25% more on your salary each year — the B.A. would be stamped by the Government on your job card. If you got an M.A., you'd get 50% more on your salary and if it was a Ph.D., you would get 100% more.

If you have, say, 80 people, you would need almost 60 jobs, thus leaving some members of each family who are free to solve problems. Each "year" lasts approximately 15 minutes, with a

5-minute break in between before the next year begins, when the family may plan for the next year, look at the next year's list of problems and work out who is going to solve them. This is also time for counting money and for going to the bank where all salaries are paid. Thus, the bank has to have a great supply of play money. Occasionally, you may hit the families with taxes as well and they have to pay the Government a certain amount, a percentage of their income, or something for taxes. You can run the game for 5-15 minute "years" and the family that comes out economically the best is the winner.

It is important to be fair when you are handing out the jobs at the beginning of the game, to make sure that the higher-paying jobs such as doctors and lawyers and dentists are spread evenly among the families so that no family has a tremendous advantage to begin with. Normally there should be 3 or 4 doctor jobs, 3 or 4 dentists, etc., so that there will be a good deal of competition in bidding between members of a profession to solve problems. This keeps the prices down and provides a lot of entertainment; however, you may have several professions where there are only 1 or 2 jobs available, such as garbage collectors, funeral directors and ministers, and this almost creates a monopoly for certain families, with prices skyrocketing. You may want to do this as it makes the game much more entertaining. This game may fit well into a later discussion on the family and enable you to talk about exclusive and inclusive families and the whole problem of competition in our society. "Do unto others as you would have them do unto you" becomes a very real principle when you realize that what you charge for your plumbing job, you may also get charged for when you are burying a loved one.

THE GOLD RUSH

This is a rather elaborate camp game. It may be used during a whole afternoon and evening. The entire camp is turned into a kind of boom town, with the Sheriff's office, Assayer's Office, Henrietta's Hash House, Mayor's home, Jail, Claims Office, etc.

The camp should be divided into 9 teams. Each is given a map of the forest around the camp which is divided into 9 claims. They are told to decide on which one they want to mine. Did they want the largest claim or the smallest? The closest to the Jail or not? The one closest to the other claims, or one off by itself? On each claim hide about 75-100 pieces of gold (rocks of varying sizes painted gold). Each piece of gold has the claim number on it, e.g., the gold on Claim #3 has a "3" on it. The gold may be hidden under logs, put on tree limbs — some just scattered in the thickest brush. The claims should be dense forest at least 100 x 50 yards wide. They should also be clearly marked either by trails or toilet paper strung out through the trees.

All the teams then meet in a clearing and select a runner to run for them to the Claims Office to stake the claim they want. Begin the race with a gunshot, and the runners then race to stake their claim — first come, first served — the last one getting what is left over. After being given the claim slip at the Claims Office they run back to their areas and begin hunting for gold. Each team is given a number of potato sacks in which to store its gold. They have to keep all their gold on their claim till the end of the game. After twenty minutes of mining their claim, a bell is rung and the teams are now allowed to "jump" other claims, either to search for gold not yet found, or to raid the main stockpile of another team. Incentive to claim jump may be given by saying that you will award a team double the points for gold with another team's claim number on it.

Each team may defend its claim by using water guns filled with water tinted with red food coloring. Give each team six water guns and two pails of red water. All claim jumpers must wear a colored team arm band to identify themselves. They can only shoot on another's claim, not on any trail or road dividing the claims. If one team manages to get some red on a claim jumper they blow a whistle and the sheriff or one of his deputies (the camp work crew or leadership) comes to the scene. All wounded claim jumpers must cooperate once they are shot and are taken by the sheriff's men to the prison — two large concentric circles of flour about 20 to 10 yards in diameter. The space between the outer and inner circle is "no man's land," while the inner circle is the jail itself where the prisoners are kept. Several deputies patrol the prison circumference with water guns and watch for people trying to break prisoners out.

When a prisoner is brought in, put a big O on one cheek in indelible ink to indicate he is a prisoner; his team number is recorded along with his name. His team must break him out within twenty minutes of his arrest — by sending a man to run into the prison to touch him, whereupon both are free to leave. A person trying to break someone out of Jail may not be shot by a deputy till he enters the clearly marked "no man's land." He is safe if he reaches the inner circle without being shot. If he is shot, he too is made a prisoner and his team number recorded. However, if a man is freed from prison by a comrade, he still has an "O" on his cheek and may be shot by "bounty hunters" because he is now a fugitive from justice. He may be shot on any trail or road or any claim except his own and the team shooting him is given $1,000 at the end of the game for bringing him back to the Jail.

If a team fails to break one of their men out of Jail before the 20 minutes is up, the prisoner is released and a big "O" painted on the back of his hand to show he has been properly released. However, his team is charged $2,000 bail for his release. He may not be shot by bounty hunters because of the "O" on his hand. However, if he is shot claim jumping again, an "O" will be put on the other cheek, etc., etc. Thus it generally pays to break your men out of jail.

Allow the claim jumping to go on for about an hour. Then ring the bell and the game is over. At the end of the game each team brings all its gold into the Assayer's Office where it is carefully stored till after supper.

The evening is ended by having the Assayer, with the sheriff guarding him, weigh up all the gold (doubling the weight of stolen gold). He then writes out a check for the amount of gold and the team leader cashes this at the nearby Bank. The Banker may pay off any way he wants — in chocolate bars or other kinds of food. (How about stacks of chocolate coins covered in gold wrapping?) You may also "double-cross" the teams somewhat by having some of the gold thrown out by the Assayer as fool's gold. How can he distinguish? All the coins have numbers on them — those with numbers in green are true gold; those with numbers in blue are fool's gold.

THE HUDSON'S BAY VS. NORTHWEST FUR TRADING COMPANY

Start with an outline of the history of the battle for fur trading territory between these two companies. The two teams are given adjacent territory and different colored armbands to distinguish them. Clearly mark the dividing line between territories. The object of the game is for each team to find "furs" on their own territory and deliver them to their headquarters in the other's territory. Thus the "voyageurs" must carry a load of furs (up to 10 each) across the line through enemy territory to the safety of their post (a natural clearing, large circle, camp shelter, etc.). Once they cross into enemy territory they may be "killed" by the other team and their furs seized.

The "furs" may be strips of cardboard 2" x 6" long or pieces of wood of the same length. Spread about 200 pieces all through each territory. All the Hudson's Bay fur should be marked with an "H" and spread in their territory; all the Northwest fur should be with an "N" and spread in their territory.

Instruct the teams that they may search for furs on their own territory and then deliver them to their headquarters — or they could send men into enemy territory to hunt for fur and deliver it to their headquarters. Of course, as soon as a person crosses the line he may be "killed" (i.e. his armband ripped off by the enemy). No fur could be taken into a headquarters by a person missing his armband. If you are "killed" you must surrender any fur you have to the enemy and return to your own lines to pick up a new armband and start again.

This game is very effective in brush country — particularly in winter or at night because the fur is easily hidden — and it involves a lot of "skulking." The center boundary line must be clearly marked especially at night; a couple of bonfires would be sufficient. The game is stopped at an arbitrary time limit (such as ¾ of an hour) and the furs counted to see who won. To encourage risking your "life," team may be awarded double points for every enemy fur they deliver to their headquarters. Give 100 points for every fur of their own delivered, 200 for every enemy fur delivered.

KAMIKAZE

This is an outdoor game, good for camps or any group of thirty or more people. Divide the group into two teams. One team will be identified by blue and the other by gold. These colors may be indicated with armbands. Each team has a "president" who may only be assassinated by a water balloon. The president is seated in a chair which is inside a four foot circle. This chair is in the center of a larger circle, some thirty or forty feet in diameter.

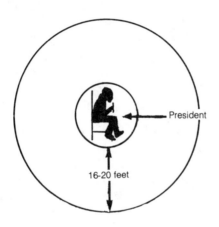

Each team has the same setup for its own president in two different locations. Both teams have offensive and defensive players. The offensive players each get two water balloons and may move in any part of the boundaries except for the area which composes the two circles with the president in the center. No person (offensive or defensive) may enter or pass through the two circles which surround the president.

The offensive players try to assassinate the president of the opposite team. They do this by tossing underhanded, a water bomb (balloon), from the edge of the outer circle. The toss must have an arch in it. If the balloon hits below the waist of the president, he is merely wounded and it takes three "wound" shots to assassinate him. A balloon hitting on target (above the waist) kills the president and the game is over (or if not over, points are scored and the team elects a new president . . .). A "judge" should be on hand to determine the legality of shots.

Defensive players are armed with a small paper bag of flour. Obviously, their job is to defend the president. They may "kill" the other team's offensive players by breaking the bag of flour on them, thus getting flour all over them. Offensive players may not kill defensive players. They simply must run back into their own territory. Defensive players are not allowed into the other team's territory. (The playing area should be divided in half, with each team's president located in his own half of the total playing area.) When a defensive player kills an offensive player, he takes his armband and the dead offensive player must go to the graveyard and is out of the game. When all of the offensive players of a team are killed, they automatically lose the game.

The game is over either after a time limit or when the president is assassinated. However, to prevent the game from being over too soon, it might be best to simply call a time-out when the president is assassinated and let the teams have five minutes or so to reorganize, elect a new president, get their dead players back in the game, and then resume the game. Also, during the break, scores are taken by the scorekeeper. Assassination of the president is worth 200 points and armbands of enemy players killed are worth 50 points each. New water balloons and flour sacks are passed out during each break (if any), which follows a president's assassination.

There should be at least four adult judges: One judge each for the team play areas and one judge to watch each president. Another person should be on hand to pass out flour sacks and balloons. (If a player uses up his supply at any time, he can go and get more.) This ammo area is "safe" and no fighting may be done there.

PIKE'S PEAK

Divide the group in half. Each team chooses a captain. Both captains are then stranded on "Pike's Peak" which is located 200-300 yards from "Pike's Dam" (water source). Each captain is holding an empty gallon container. Each team member is given a small Dixie Cup. The object is to fill the cup with water at Pike's Dam (the only water source allowed) and to fill the captain's container. The first team to have a completely full container wins. The object is to stop the other team before they get to the captain by spilling their water, or throwing water all over them.

Rules:

1. Boys may get boys, but boys may not get girls. (They can run, but no offense.)

2. Girls may get both guys and girls.

3. Within two feet of the captain is a "free zone" and no combat may take place there.

4. It's best to have neutral people at the dam to fill the cups and have each team fill at opposite ends of the water source.

5. Distinguish teams with colored tape on their foreheads (or any marking device).

SMUGGLER

This is a great camp game. It is relatively complicated and requires the use of the entire camp area (several acres or so). There are two teams (any number on a team), two "territories" (divide the camp in half) and each team should be appropriately marked (colored armbands, etc.). The idea of the game is to smuggle certain items into the other team's territory successfully (without being captured) and make a "drop." Points are awarded for successful drops and for capturing smugglers.

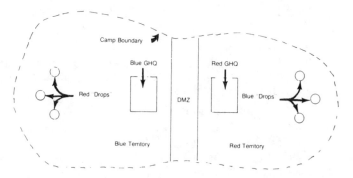

Teams should have names or be designated by color (i.e. Red Army, Blue Army). Each team selects up to 25 percent of its players (number can vary) to be "smugglers." They are so identified with an "S" marked on the back of their hands with a felt-tipped pen. They are the only ones who are allowed to smuggle items into the other team's territory. The rest of the team may capture smugglers from the other team. Smugglers may not capture anyone. Each team should also have a "general" who is "in charge," coordinates team strategy, and remains at all times in the "GHQ" (General's headquarters).

Camp staff and counselors are neutral and are called "U.N. Observers." They are positioned on the two teams' territories to maintain order, offer advice, and make sure everyone is playing by the rules of the game. One U.N. Observer on each side should be assigned the task of keeping score for that side.

One interesting twist to this game is to allow a certain number of "infiltrators" or spies to wear the armbands of one team, but they are actually working for the other team. They may be chosen by the game officials prior to the game and secretly informed of their mission. Infiltrators are secretly marked with an "X" (or anything) on one leg (or some other place that is relatively hidden). If a player is accused of being an infiltrator, he must show his leg, and tell the truth. If the accusation is correct, the accusing team gets 5,000 points and the infiltrator is taken into custody. He must remain in the GHQ for 10 minutes and is then released to the team for whom he is working. He gets a new armband and is back in the game, only not as an infiltrator. An incorrect accusation costs the accusing team 5,000 points (points lost). Note: Only the general of each team may make an accusation. If a player suspects that a teammate is a spy, the general is informed and he decides whether or not to accuse. Then the accusation must be made in the presence of a U.N. Observer.

The "drops" are locations (under rocks, in trees, etc.) where a smuggled item may be placed, upon which it may be declared successfully smuggled. Only the smuggling team knows where all the drops are in the opposing team's territory.

However, before the game begins, each team locates their drop positions in the other team's territory, and a game official (neutral person) informs the opposing team's general as to the location of half of them. So, the blue team, for example, might know where half of the red team's drops are, and the red team isn't sure which ones they know about. There should be at least four drops for each side (any number without getting ridiculous). U.N. Observers should know where all the drop locations are.

The "DMZ" is a neutral area marked off between the two territories. Anyone may be there without being captured. This is good for strategy, but may be optional.

The game should be played at night. No flashlights are allowed. Because the entire camp is used, buildings, trees, and other obstacles may be used for cover. Unsafe areas should be declared off limits. Players caught in an off-limits area should be penalized by subtracting 5,000 points from their team's score.

The items to be smuggled are simply 3 x 5 cards with the name of the item on it and its value.

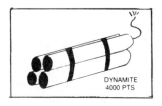

DYNAMITE
4000 PTS

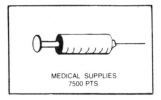

MEDICAL SUPPLIES
7500 PTS

Different items are worth more than others. Points should range anywhere from 1,000 points to 10,000 points. There should be more items of lower point value with the high scoring items being more "rare." Any number of items may be used in the game, as long as each team has the same number with the same values. The red team's items should be written in red ink, and vice-versa.

As the game progresses, smugglers attempt to get items behind enemy lines and successfully "dropped" at one of the drop locations in enemy territory. Only one item may be smuggled at a time by a smuggler. Once a drop is made (successfully), the smuggler raises his hand and yells "U.N." until he finds or is found by a U.N. Observer. The U.N. Observer then verifies the drop and escorts him back to his own territory where points are awarded. While a smuggler has his hand raised and is yelling "U.N.," he may not be captured by the enemy. Faking this procedure is a rule infraction that costs you 5,000 points.

If the smuggler is captured during his smuggling attempt, he is brought to the GHQ of the capturing team and must remain there for 10 minutes before being released. (This time may vary.) He also gets a mark on his hand in the capturing team's color.

In the face of imminent capture, a smuggler may dump or get rid of the item he is attempting to smuggle and hope that it will not be discovered or that it might be picked up by a fellow smuggler. If the capturing team finds it, they may turn it in for its face value.

Smugglers may be captured any number of ways, depending on how rough or messy you want to get. They may be tagged, tackled, hit with a water balloon, or perhaps hit with a nylon stocking full of flour. Choose your own method.

Scoring:

1. A successful drop is worth 1,000 points plus the value of the item.

2. An extra 2,000 points is earned if the smuggler can make a successful drop and return to his own team's territory

without being captured by the enemy or escorted back by a U.N. Observer.

3. On capturing a smuggler, the capturing team gets points in the following manner:

   a. First time caught — 500 points plus half the value of the item being smuggled.

   b. Second time caught — 1500 points plus full value of item.

   c. Third time caught — 3000 points plus full value of item.

4. Correctly identifying an infiltrator is worth 5000 points. Incorrectly accusing one costs 5000 points.

5. Any "item" found bearing the opposing team's color may be turned in for the full value of the item.

SPY GAME

This game is great for week-long camps. The spies should be chosen early in the camp (by the end of first full day) and much should be made of suspicions of who spies are. There is no way for the campers to be sure who the spies are until the game — but different ones may be accused of it all week long.

The bomb designation site should be out of the main traffic area — but still reachable by any means available to the campers.

One person should serve as referee. It could be the camp director since he has chosen all the spies. Rules and objectives of game should be explained at earliest possible meeting of the camp.

SPIES:

Selection:

Made by Camp Director secretly.

Not more than 25 or ¼ of total camp

May be staff and/or campers

Must be selected before head cops are elected

One must serve as Head Spy

Must be informed secretly at beginning of week

Meetings:

Must be secret when members not missed

Should meet at least once during week or as many times as necessary not arousing suspicion but allowing effective plan

Head Spy calls meeting — must be done individually

Before first meeting no one but Head Spy knows who the others are

Objective:

To place bomb in designated area during time allowed which will "blow up the camp"

COPS:

Selection:

All campers and counselors are cops (even those who have been selected as spies)

Each cabin group is to elect one cop to represent them on Cop Council to plan strategy

One Cop selected as Chief Cop by Council from its members

Meetings of Cop Council:

May meet openly and as often as necessary to lay plans for defense

Chief Cop calls meetings

Objective:

To capture bomb during time limit before it is placed in designated area

BOMB:

Made by Camp Director in such a way to be known by him as actual bomb

May be duplicated secretly by spies but there can be only one bomb

Kept on display during week

Prison Area:

> 40-foot diameter circle. No closer than 30 yards from bomb designated area, nor farther than 100 yards
>
> To contain spies who have been caught
>
> Release of spies before time expires may only be by another spy who is free

Bomb Designated Area:

> A stationary object during game such as truck building, etc. with 500 foot diameter circle around object
>
> Only spies may enter area and only when they have the bomb or after bomb goes into bomb designated area
>
> Cops may not enter under any circumstances

Capture of Spies:

> Spies can only be captured and imprisoned during designated time and only then after badge has been discovered on their discretionary person
>
> The only way to prove a person is a spy is to discover a spy badge on his person

Spy Badges:

> Size — no larger than 3 x 5
> no smaller than 1 x 2
>
> Must have SPY written on it
>
> May be given to spies no sooner than day before game
>
> Must be hidden on their discreet person — no embarrassing searches may be made

Time Schedule:

> All campers assemble in one room and rules are clarified (may be done during any one hour segment)
>
> 2:00 One Spy revealed to take bomb
>
> 2:05 Cops released from room
>
> 2:20 Bomb may be placed

3:00 Game ends if bomb is not captured before this time or if the camp has not been blown off the face of the earth

Note: a predetermined spy must admit his identity and come forward to receive the bomb to start the game

Boundaries:

No one may leave camp property — either to hide the bomb or to search for it

WAR

The following game is great for camps or retreats where there is plenty of room to play (like several areas of rugged terrain). Any number may play. The entire crowd is divided up into two "armies," the "Red Army" and the "Black Army." (You may come up with more creative names for the armies if you prefer.) Each army has a "general" (a leader) and is identified by red or black armbands, which may not be removed during the game.

The object of the game is to destroy the opponent's "radar installation." This is done by dropping a "bomb" on it, which will be explained in detail later.

Both armies are divided up into two units: the "offensive" and the "defensive." The offensive unit's mission is to seek and destroy the opponent's radar installation, and is under the command of a "colonel." The offensive unit is also divided into "platoons" of from five to seven members each. Each platoon has a "captain" and a "lieutenant" who is second in command in each platoon. The offensive unit has no boundary restrictions. These players may go anywhere to accomplish their mission.

The defensive unit of each army has the same organization as the offensive unit (with the same leadership and platoons), but the mission is to protect its own radar station and to repel the invading offensive unit of the opposing army. This unit may not enter the territory of the other army.

Each army should, by the way, have its own "territory." Half the playing area should be assigned to each army and marked appropriately.

The "radar installations" are two containers (preferably

brightly colored) placed on the ground somewhere in each of the two armies' territories. They cannot be camouflaged or hidden. They must be easily visible to the opposing army once the opposing army gets near to it. Any type container will do.

Each army gets a certain number of "bombs" (25 or so). A "live" bomb is a plastic bottle (or any small container) containing a jelly bean that is the color of the respective army. A "deactivated" bomb is a plastic bottle without a jelly bean. Only the offensive units of each army are allowed to carry bombs. In order to destroy the opponent's radar installation, a *live* bomb must be dropped into it. The defensive soldiers may seize bombs from their opponents and deactivate them by destroying the jelly bean (eating it). The captured bomb may then be "activated" by the capturing team with a new jelly bean of its own color, making its own army a little stronger. (The more bombs an army has, the better chance it has of getting one into the opposing army's radar station successfully.)

Other weapons are used in the game as well. Guns are felt-tipped pens. Generals and colonels have two each. Each captain has one for his platoon. No other players may carry guns. Guns may also be captured from opposing players.

To "shoot" an opponent, he must first be captured. Capturing a player is done simply by grabbing him and holding him down (overpowering him). Boys may capture boys, but boys may not capture girls. Girls, on the other hand, may capture anyone that they wish. Anything goes in the capturing process. A captured player is then "shot" by having one finger of the left hand marked with a felt-tipped pen (gun). The opponent is then released. He may not be pursued for two minutes, or re-captured by anyone for two minutes. Also, he may not attack the radar station or one of his opponents for the same length of time. A player is "dead" and out of the game when he has had four fingers on his left hand marked (shot four times). He then must report to the camp and remain there until the game is over. (If you prefer, you may "recycle" dead players by allowing them to wait ten minutes, then marking a big "purple heart" or some other identification on the palm of their left hand. After that they may return to the game. They can then be "shot" four more times on their right hand.)

The game is over when either radar has been bombed three times with a live bomb. At that point a signal will be sounded and all the players must return to the center of the camp. The losing general surrenders to the opposing general.

This game may be changed or adapted as you see fit. It may be played with more than two armies as well. Playing time is usually about an hour or so, including time for each army to get organized.

THE WATERGATE GAME

This game has been named after the famous Washington scandal, but it may be re-named if used after the Watergate event has vanished from the American scene or if it is considered to be in poor taste. The important thing is the fun of playing the game. However, the play can become more intense when associated with a famous event such as Watergate. The game may be played with any number of players (20 or so) and is designed as an indoor game, utilizing several rooms.

The basic theme of the game is this: certain security agents of the FBI are allowed to see and hear a number of tapes connected with Watergate. They are only allowed to see and hear these in a top secret room in the White House, off the White House Library. Any top secret FBI man is allowed into the White House Library and into the special room where he can hear tapes. However, he is not allowed to leave the White House without being searched by security police. The security police are not allowed to go out of the White House Library into the special room where the tapes are heard by the FBI agents. The FBI is under instructions to obtain a certain number of these tapes containing certain conversations that the Watergate Committee wishes to hear and the Department of Justice wishes to obtain. They must then systematically examine all of the tapes from the library in this special room and decide which ones they wish to try to smuggle out of the White House. If they wish to smuggle a tape out of the White House, they take it out of its envelope or box, whichever is being used, and replace it with something of the same size and shape and weight.

They turn in the substitute at the library and take the tape itself and place it in a suitcase or bag or knapsack or whatever, in amongst clothes or whatever people want to carry in the bags. They then seek to leave the White House by one of say, 5 or 6 different doors. The White House security police are allowed to search half of the luggage of a person leaving the White House. This means that you have every FBI agent either carrying two or four pieces of luggage and only 1 or 2 pieces may be searched as they leave. The other half of their luggage represents their person and may only be searched if the person is first arrested and taken to the special police station room off the White House Library. Thus, if a White House security agent decided a person is really suspicious and should have all of his luggage checked, he can place his hand upon that person's shoulder and put him under arrest, taking him to a police station right within the White House, where the agent is turned in and must admit whether or not he has a tape on him. If he does have, he must turn it in and the White House security police collects 35,000 points for having seized the tape. If, on the other hand, the FBI man does not have a tape in his possession, the White House security police lose 10,000 points for falsely arresting an agent. In either case, the agent is set free as soon as he has been questioned by police. It becomes obvious, then, that once an FBI agent is turned in to the police station, he must tell the truth or the whole game breaks down.

If the security police manage to find a tape in a suitcase, as someone is leaving, they don't bother arresting the fellow, they just seize the tape and turn it in at the police station, thus receiving another 35,000 points for their vigilance.

You will need a large number of "tapes" in the White House Library. One group used empty cassettes with empty tapes, another used home movies and home movie boxes. Another used small plastic pill bottles in brown paper bags. There should be a number on the bag or box on the outside and the same number on a piece of masking tape on the actual tape, film or pill bottle. There should also be a note stuck on the tape stating the contents of that particular tape, i.e., "Meeting between Nixon and Dean, Nov. 21, 1972," etc. The FBI is given a list of about 40 tapes they are to seize, (that is, they are given a list of the contents of 40 meetings they are to secure). The game runs for about 30 to 35 minutes and then breaks for 10 minutes in the middle, where you may reorganize and the people who were the security police become the FBI agents and the FBI agents become security police for the second half.

One group added a variation which made the game much more interesting. These were approximately 80 people playing the game, 40 on each team. They therefore made up 40 pieces of paper for each half, neatly folded over, and on about 6 of them wrote down a combination password, for instance a statement that an FBI agent would make, such as: "It's been a lousy day, hasn't it?," with a reply by the White House security police to the effect that: "It's been lousy ever since Nov. 1st." They had each White House security policeman draw one piece of paper, keep it to himself and get a chance to look at it as soon as he could without anyone else around. If he found, on his piece of paper, a set of statements to be used as a password, he knew he was a collaborator, a double agent, who was actually working for the FBI although he was on the White House security police staff.

Every collaborator was to seek to try to help the FBI get tapes out of the White House. The main way of doing this, of course, was simply to be stationed at one of the doors, to somehow contact the FBI and let them know they were collaborators and then to help them go through their station by searching their suitcases and letting them go through if they did find a tape. The collaborators' main problem was that they did not know who else was a collaborator and who was not. Therefore, they had to be very careful lest they be caught by their own security force. Their situation was made even more difficult by the fact that every time the FBI was able to use a collaborator, they had to pay them (we gave every FBI agent some phony $1,000 bills that they were to give to a collaborator who helped them). The money had to be given to the collaborator within 3 minutes of his helping an agent. Thus, every collaborator had to be very careful he was not spotted receiving cash from the FBI. If a White House security policeman suspected that one of his colleagues was a collaborator, he could arrest him and turn him in at the police station. At the police station, they were interviewed and if they were collaborators, they went over and started working for the FBI. The White House security police received 100,000 points for catching a collaborator. If, on the other hand, he was not a collaborator, they would lose 10,000 points for falsely arresting one of their own men, and that man would be back to work for them.

Further pressure was put on the collaborators as follows: if, at half time, when they were asked to confess whether or not they were collaborators, they admitted to being collaborators but had not received any money from the FBI, then the FBI would lose 50,000 points. Thus, every collaborator, if he really wanted to help his team, had to get a contact with them. He had to be of some use to them and get paid for it.

This game may be run with one team simply the FBI and one team as the White House security police, but generally the players like to play both sides.

This game may be used in conjunction with a discussion on "Honesty," in which you may consider much wider issues of both public and private honesty, particularly "Why am I afraid to be honest?"

WELLS FARGO

This game is best at a camp or wherever there is plenty of running room, terrain, trees, and good places to hide. It is also best with more than 50 people, and may be played with as many as a thousand. It can be a dangerous game, resulting in injuries unless there is strict enforcement of the rules and every safety precaution taken. But the risk is usually worth it, as the game is one of the most exciting camp games ever created.

Divide the entire group into two teams, the Cowboys and the Indians. Indian headbands, war paint, cowboy hats, etc. help to make the game more fun, but are not necessary. In the center of an open field, mark off an 8 by 8 foot area which becomes the "bank." A large garbage can may be used as the bank, if you prefer. You will also need to prepare a number of "bags of gold." These may be potato sacks filled with rocks. They should be light enough to be carried by one person, or tossed from one person to another. You will also need a piece of tape for each person. These are stuck on each one's forehead and become their "scalps." (It is safer, however, to place the tapes on their arms rather than their foreheads.) It is best to use two different colors of tape to distinguish the Cowboys from the Indians, but you may simply mark the pieces of tape with X's and O's. Each player must wear his scalp so that it can be easily seen. Scalps may not be hidden under hats, hair, clothing, and the like.

To start the game, the Cowboys get the gold and have ten minutes to hide out in the woods or wherever, and at a signal, the Indians are released to try to find them. There are two objectives to the game: (1) To get the gold, or in the Cowboys' case, to get the gold into the bank, and (2) to get scalps (tape). The Cowboys try to get the gold in the bank, because if they don't, they don't get credit for it. If the Indians can capture it by overpowering the Cowboys who have it, it becomes theirs and the Cowboys may not get it back. As a safety measure, boys may not attack or scalp girls, but girls *can* attack and scalp boys. It is best for players to travel in groups and work out their strategies. Cowboys may scalp Indians as well as vice-versa. Once you are scalped, you are "dead," and must go to boot hill. You are out of the game.

The bags of gold are worth 1000 points each. Cowboys must get their bag into the bank. It is worthless to them if they still have it in their possession at the end of the game.

The Indians don't have to put it in the bank to collect their points. All they have to do is capture it and stash it someplace until the game is over. The scalps are worth 100 points each. The game may last 30 to 45 minutes or so, and at the end of the game the teams add up their scores, based on how many scalps they have and how many bags of gold they have in the bank or captured. The team with the most points wins.

WORLD WAR

This is a fun game for groups of over fifty. It is excellent for camps and may be followed up the next day with a "total disarmament" game or "cease-fire" game which involves feeding the hungry, clothing the naked, or whatever. The purpose of this game is simply to win the war. This is done by destroying the enemy and capturing or killing their general.

Necessary Props:

(1) Water balloons. These are used as bombs, mortar shells, hand grenades, etc.

(2) Armbands of various colors to identify everyone. For example, have a red army versus a blue army, by using appropriate colored bands on the right arm. Also another color of armband may be used on the left arm to signify whether the person is air force, artillery, etc.

(3) Plenty of room to play (do battle) with good hiding places and such.

(4) Non-military supervisors to make sure all the rules of the game are being followed. These people have the power to kill or heal at will. They should be equipped with whistles to start and stop the game, call violations, etc.

(5) An area marked off for the military graveyard.

Personnel Involved and Their Roles:

(1) "General." Each army has one. He wears either a red or blue armband (depending on his army), plus a bright yellow band across his chest (Miss America style). He is the commander-in-chief. He may be killed by having his armband or his general's band ripped off. He cannot be killed by mortars, bombs, grenades, etc. (The idea here is that the generals are usually well protected in bunkers, not susceptible to artillery attack or strafing. They must be killed or captured only in hand-to-hand combat.)

(2) "Air Force." These are the only people in the game allowed to run. Everyone else walks. (The non-military supervisors carefully enforce this. Violators have their

armbands removed and are sent to the military graveyard.) Air force people wear their bands on their right arms and a sky-blue band on their left arms. They may only carry two water balloons at a time. (Any air force person with more than two bombs is sent to the graveyard.) Air force may run in and out of any situation with two bombs. They may strafe any person except generals. (Anyone with water on him is considered "dead.") Air force may also run up to any person, take off either armband, and run away. If the armband, which represents artillery, air force, etc., is taken, but the armband signifying either red or blue army remains, that person becomes infantry. (Note: To capture a general, air force may run into general's bunker, tear off the air force insignia from his own arm, thus becoming a paratrooper. Once the air force insignia is off, however, the person may only walk and may carry no bombs.)

(3) "Artillery." These soldiers may only walk and are identified by a green armband on the left arm and a red or blue band on the right arm. They are allowed as many water balloons as they can carry and may attack anyone with them. They can also function as refilling (rearming) stations for the air force. Once their artillery insignia is torn off, however, they may no longer touch the water balloons, even to hide or destroy them.

(4) "Infantry." These are the backbone of the armies. They only wear a red or blue band. They may only walk, but can kill anyone they come across. They should be used to protect the artillery and the generals.

Further Instructions:

(1) Bombs and cannon shells (water balloons) are lethal to anyone who gets wet from them, including the thrower.

(2) Infantry may destroy the enemy supply of balloons by poking them with a stick. They may not, however, pick them up for any reason.

(3) Game ends when one general is either killed or captured.

(4) You may make the game interesting by setting sprinklers

going here and there as mine fields. You may also rope off strategic paths as "radioactive" and anyone entering the area is dead and sent to the graveyard.

(5) Once dead, the person may not kill anyone, and may not divulge any information.

SCAVENGER HUNTS

SCAVENGER HUNTS

COMPARISON SCAVENGER HUNT

This is a good game for camps and outdoor activities. Instead of having a "normal" scavenger hunt, where everyone goes out and brings back specific items on a list, have groups go out and bring back things like:

1. The biggest piece of wood they can find
2. The oldest nickel
3. The smelliest sock
4. The heaviest rock
5. The most worn-out shoe (or tire)
6. The rustiest tin can
7. The ugliest picture
8. The biggest leaf
9. The largest book

Have the kids bring back all the stuff and then one at a time bring each item up for comparison. The group with the "biggest," "oldest," etc. on each team gets points awarded for each item. Arrange for a panel of "judges" who inspect each item and choose the winners.

CRAZY CREATIVE SCAVENGER HUNT

Here's a fun variation of the old scavenger hunt. Give each team a list of crazy names (such as the following sample list) and the kids have to go out and collect items that they think *best fit* the names on the list. For example:

1. A P B J
2. Zipper zapping shoestring fuse
3. Idaho
4. Tweed
5. Snail Egg
6. Chicken Lips
7. Will be
8. Pine Needle Bushing Brush
9. Snipe
10. Piano Key Mustache Waxer
11. G-Branded Breast Boxers
12. Yellow Grot Grabber
13. Portable Electric Door Knob Kneeler
14. Thumb Twiddly Dummer
15. Thingamabob
16. An Inflatable Deflater
17. Galvanized Goul Gooser

A panel of judges can determine the winners based on each team's explanation of how their "items" fit the various descriptions on the list.

INDOOR TREASURE HUNT

This is a good indoor game for Junior High. Twenty-five objects are placed in plain sight in various places around the room or rooms available. (If in a home, use several rooms.) Attached to each object is a number. Each person is given a list (like the one below) and the idea is to find the objects on the list, write in the numbers attached, and be the first one to do so. No one may move or touch an object when it is found, but simply record the number attached to it. A sample list:

1. Match
2. Stocking
3. Needle and thread
4. Thimble

5. Straight pin
6. Glass button
7. Paper clip
8. White string
9. Penny
10. Dime
11. Dollar bill
12. Bracelet
13. Ring
14. Bobby pin
15. Postage stamp
16. Paper reinforcement
17. Paper fastener (brad)
18. Ribbon
19. Toothpick
20. Garter
21. Safety pin
22. Door key
23. Rubber band
24. Stick of gum — don't chew it!
25. Earring

HALLOWEEN SCAVENGER HUNT

If you can locate an old-out-of-the-way (deserted) cemetery, here's a spooky Halloween Party idea. Get permission from the cemetery custodians or director to have a "scavenger hunt." Make a list of names found on tombstones and have the kids try to locate them and write in the dates found on the tombstone on the list. The most complete list of names and dates wins. Do it at night, and provide flashlights. Be sure to let the police and neighbors know what's going on.

INDOOR SCAVENGER HUNT

Divide the group into teams. Each team gets into one corner of the room with you in the middle. Each team appoints a "runner" who runs items from the team to you. You call out various items that might be in the group, and each team tries to locate that item among team members, then gives it to the runner. He then runs it to you. The first team to produce the named item wins 100 points, and after 20 or so items, the team with the most points wins. Make sure that the runners all are running approximately the same distance. Some sample items that you can call out:

A white comb	A turquoise ring or bracelet
A red sock	The smelliest sock you can find
A 1969 penny	(judge to decide the winner)
A student body card	A stick of gum
An eyelash curler	A theater ticket
Four belts all tied together	Toenail clippers
Dark glasses	A book of matches
Picture of a rock star	A cowboy boot
A twenty-dollar bill	Forty-six cents exactly
Some beef jerky	A handkerchief
Denture adhesive	A Timex watch
A hat	A book with no pictures

MAKE A PIZZA NIGHT

Divide kids into small groups (3-5), then give each group a pizza dough shell (the frozen kind). Send them out in a residential area with a time limit (60-90 minutes) and no money. They must beg the necessary items (sauce, cheese, etc.), and use of oven to make the pizza. Scoring can include quickest back, best tasting, most items (points may be assigned to certain items — 3 for hot peppers, 2 for sausage, etc). All that is needed when they get back is cool drinks.

MANHUNT

This is really a "people scavenger hunt," in that the game is played just like a scavenger hunt, only the object of the hunt is people. The group meets at a central location and is divided up into teams. Each team is then given a list of people (not names) to "bring back alive" to the meeting to be held later in the evening. The teams then go out into the neighborhood (in cars or on foot). They try to locate people to fit the descriptions on the list, and also try to talk each person into coming back to the meeting with them. No one may be forced into coming. Each person is worth 100 points. Here is a sample list:

A varsity football player
An A.S.B. officer
Someone who speaks Spanish
A tuba player (with tuba)
Someone who weighs over 200 pounds
A cheerleader
A girl with her hair in rollers
A couple who are "going steady"
A guy in his pajamas
A teacher
Someone who drives a Corvette
Someone who has more than ten letters in his last name
A girl with red hair
An "A" student
Someone who owns a guinea pig
Someone over six feet tall
Someone who plays a banjo

You may add more to this list, of course, or delete those you don't like. Give players plenty of things to choose from. The team with the most people brought in wins.

POLAROID PEOPLE PICTURES

This is a combination of two ideas: "The Human Scavenger Hunt" and "The Polaroid Scavenger Hunt." But the result is a brand new special event idea which provides the best of both. Here's how it works: Have the group meet on a Saturday morning around nine or ten o'clock. Divide the group into teams and give each a "Swinger" type Polaroid camera and two rolls of film. Each team is also given a list of subjects to be shot which involve people. No one from the group may be in the picture; only total strangers may be used. Each team must work in the same general vicinity, as well, such as the zoo, the park, downtown, etc. People may be asked to pose for the pictures. A sample list:

1. Bad ecology
2. Someone disappointed
3. Compassion
4. Someone showing love
5. Someone asleep on a bench
6. Old man and a young child
7. Cruelty
8. Policeman doing his job
9. Someone showing courtesy
10. A dog
11. Child with a balloon

The group is given a time limit and the pictures are judged to select a winning team. The pictures may be mounted for display or be used for discussion as well.

POLAROID POSERS SCAVENGER HUNT

This is a great idea for a party or social that is really different. The idea is to divide your group into teams of five or six people each. Each team is given a Polaroid Camera, two packages of film (8 exposures each), an hour or two of daylight, and a list of pictures to be taken. The teams all go out in cars and must take at least 15 pictures chosen from the list within the time limit. The pictures are given point values rated according to difficulty, and the team accumulating the most points, wins. The following list of rules and directions should be given to each team:

The Rules:

A. This is a contest between teams to see which team can accumulate the greatest number of points. Points are earned by taking pictures, as described below, of everyone on the team. The point values of each picture are indicated by the number in parenthesis at the end of each picture description.

B. All teams will leave the group's parking lot at the same

time, equipped with 1) a Polaroid camera, 2) a team photographer, and 3) an impartial supervisor-driver.

C. Each team must pick a team name and a team captain. The team captain will determine where the team is to go to take the pictures.

D. All arrangements for all pictures are to be made by the team members — not by the supervisor. The job of the supervisor is to take the team where it wants to go, and take pictures when necessary. (Each supervisor is to use his own discretion with regard to bailing his team out of jail.)

E. At least five team members must be visible and identifiable in each picture, unless otherwise designated.

Directions:

Take as many of the following pictures as possible within the time limit. They are rated point-wise according to difficulty, so you will want to consider that as you decide which ones to take. The maximum you can take is 15 pictures. Good luck.

1. Hanging by knees from a tree. (1)
2. Climbing a flagpole (bottom person must be at least 3 feet off the ground). (15)
3. In a storefront window, on a main street, blowing bubble gum. (5)
4. Inside a police car, with the policeman. (15)
5. In an airplane (10) (with a stewardess + 5; with a pilot + 7)
6. In a bath tub. (10)
7. Under a lighted building at 6:22 P.M. (15)
8. Around a tombstone (5).
9. Three members of your team in a dryer in a laundromat. (10)
10. Making French fries in the kitchen of a restaurant, with the chef. (15)
11. In a boat, on the water. (10)

12. Sitting around someone's dinner table at supper. (The family may not be that of a team member.) (10)

13. All members each trying on a pair of new white tennis shoes in a department store. (15) (With store manager + 5)

14. With at least two people not in your group, in a telephone booth. Total of seven people. (15)
(5 points extra for each additional person, not from your team, you can cram in there.)

15. In a wagon. (5)

16. Fishing on a pier with a borrowed fishing pole. (10)

17. Inside an inner tube. (5)

18. Washing a car in a car wash. (10)

19. T.P.'ing a car (not the one you're in). (10)

20. Collecting candy at a home where your team is Trick-or-treating. (10)

SCAVENGER FOOD HUNT

Instead of trick or treating at Halloween time, develop a list of food items which will make up a complete meal. Divide your group into teams and go door-to-door attempting to get every-thing on the list. Each contributing family receives a small thank-you note explaining the purpose of the collection and where the food is going.

ST. PATRICK'S DAY SCAVENGER HUNT

Next St. Patrick's Day, give the following list to teams and give them 45 minutes (or so) to collect the following items from around town. Winner is the team with the most green items.

1. Green Pepper
2. Green Pear
3. Green piece of paper
4. Green lima bean
5. Green stamps
6. Four-leaf clover or shamrock
7. Green garter
8. One dollar bill (silver certificate)
9. Green pencil
10. Green turtle (live)
11. Green button
12. Green tennis shoe (left foot)
13. Green hair ribbon
14. Bottle of Jade East

15. Green toothpick
16. Green fingernail polish
17. Green bathing suit
18. Green toothbrush
19. Green palm leaf
20. Green hand soap
21. Green straw
22. Green Dixie Cup
23. Green shoelace
24. Green sweater
25. Green sucker
26. Green shirt
27. Green sock
28. Avocado
29. 7 inch green string
30. Green ink
31. Green balloon — blown-up
32. Green newspaper
33. Green flower
34. Green fish
35. Green key
36. Green onion
37. Green plastic record
38. Green book
39. One pair green sunglasses
40. Green frog (live)
41. Green petticoat
42. Green lipstick
43. Green lampshade
44. Green Ping-Pong paddle
45. Green gum
46. Green ticket stub
47. Green postage stamp (1¢)
48. Jolly green giant picture
49. Green lime
50. Green stuffed animal

MIXERS

MIXERS

ACCIDENT REPORT

Equip each person with a pencil and paper and instruct that on a given signal (i.e. two pie pans crashing together) they are to bumb shoulders with someone close. After bumping, an accident report must be filled out getting each other's name, address, phone number, grade, driver's license number, etc. This may be continued six or eight times throughout the night's activities, each time bumping someone new.

BACK SNATCHING

This is a good way to get everyone acquainted with one another. Pin a name onto each player's back (either phony names, middle names or real names if the players don't know one another.) At a given signal, each person starts copying names off the backs of the other people, while at the same time trying to keep people from copying the name on his own back. This results in a lot of twisting, turning, and trying to keep one's back from being seen. At the end of the time limit, the person with the longest list — and most complete — wins. Have the winner identify the person with the name to claim his "prize," if any.

BACK TALK

Have everyone in the group close his eyes and cross his arms over his chest. Everyone then walks around backwards, eyes remaining shut, and when another back is encountered, the following sequence takes place: Non-verbally and back to back, express hello, show anger and then make up; express happiness, indicate good-by, turn around, open eyes and see with whom the "back talk" was experienced. Move on to another person when finished and repeat. This may go on for 5 to 15 minutes.

BALLOON BUST

This is a good way to choose couples for a game like "Birdie on the Perch" or any other game that requires couples. All the girls, or half the group (whichever is best) each get a piece of paper and a balloon. Each player writes his name on the piece of paper and then puts it inside the balloon. Then blow up the balloon and tie it. All the balloons are placed in the middle of the room. On a signal, half the group (or the boys) whose names are not in the balloons, grab a balloon, pop it, read the name on the piece of paper inside, and try to locate the person whose name they have. The last couple to locate each other and sit down on the floor is the loser.

AUTOGRAPH HUNT

This is a great crowd breaker for parties or socials. Type up a copy of the list below for everyone in the group; however, no two lists should be in the same order unless the group is very large. The idea is to have everyone doing something different at the same time. Also, you are not able to tell who is winning until the game is over. The winner is the first one to complete all ten things on his list *in order.* Anyone who will not do what someone asks him to do is automatically disqualified.

1. Get ten different autographs. First, Middle, and Last names. (On the back of this sheet.)

2. Unlace someone's shoe, lace it, and tie it again. (Not your own.)

3. Get a hair over six inches long from someone's head. (Let them remove it.)

4. Get a girl to do a somersault and sign her name here.
   _____

5. Have a boy do five pushups for you and sign his name here. _____

6. Play "Ring around the Rosy" with someone and sing out loud.

7. Do twenty-five "jumping jacks" and have someone count them off for you. Have that person sign here when you have done the stunt. _____

8. Say the "Pledge of Allegiance" to the flag as loudly as you can.

9. Leapfrog over someone five times.

10. You were given a piece of bubble gum at the beginning of the race. Chew it up and blow ten bubbles. Find someone who will watch you do it and sign here when you have finished. _____

COORDINATION CHALLENGE

You must practice this before you do it with your group. The idea is to have everyone do it *with* you. It is a 1-2-3 motion, beginning by first slapping your thighs, then clapping hands, then in one motion your right hand grabs your nose and your left hand grabs your right ear.

After everyone has gotten it, switch — left hand on nose, and right hand on left ear. Then go back and forth. This is a fun way to open a meeting.

COORDINATION CLAP

This is a crowd breaker that you can use anytime, as many times as you want. It is always fun, gets good laughs, and involves everyone. The procedure is simple. You cross your hands in an up-and-down manner (vertical), and the group must clap every time your hands cross in the middle. If your hands stop and do not cross, then the audience must not clap. That is basically it. The fun is when you fake the group out by almost crossing your hands but stopping just before they do. Go fast, slow, and point out people who goof it up by giving them a penalty of some kind. You may also keep it up and when anyone goofs, he is out of the game. Keep going until there is only one person left, and give him a prize.

EYE SPY

As a mixer, give everyone four pieces of paper. Each is to list everyone in the room according to color of eyes. (blue, green, brown, gray). First one to finish wins.

FOOT SIGNING

Have five boys come to the front of the room and remove their shoes and socks. Give each a felt-tipped or ball-point pen. On a signal, the five boys run out into the crowd and see who can get the most signatures on the bottom of their feet in the time limit. No one person may sign more than three feet. Guys may use both feet. Signatures must be legible.

HUMAN BINGO

Here is a fun way to break the ice and learn everyone's name. Give each person a Bingo card (see below). The blocks are to be filled in with the name of a person who fits the clue.

Someone with a pimple	Someone with 3 brothers	Someone with blond hair at least 12" long	Someone who plays football	Someone born outside the U.S.
Someone who owns a dog	Someone who is wearing contact lenses	Someone who is bald	Someone who owns a motorcycle	Someone with red hair
An amateur photographer	Sign your own name	A foreign student	Someone who has a snake	Someone who got an A in English
Someone who has been in Canada	Someone who weighs over 200 lbs.	Someone who owns a Volkswagen	Someone who has a leather jacket	Someone who just ate at McDonald's
Someone who went to the World's Fair	Someone who weighs under 100 lbs.	Someone who owns a horse	Someone wearing blue socks	Someone who had a bad date last weekend

Directions: Fill in the blocks shown with the names of persons who fit the descriptions in each box, these persons must be present tonight. The object, of course, is to complete the Bingo Card, either vertically, horizontally, or diagonally.

The person must sign his own name. The first person to complete all five blocks gets Bingo!

I'VE GOT YOUR NUMBER

As people arrive, each gets a number to be worn in a conspicuous place on their clothes. Ahead of time, prepare lots of instructions on little slips of paper. These are placed in a box. They should be things like:

Borrow something from #1.
Introduce #2 to #7.
Have #6 get you a glass of water.
Find out #12's middle name.
Etc.

When activity begins, each person must come up to get sheet with an instruction on it. When they have completed the instruction, they come back and get a new one. At the end of the time limit, (5 minutes or so), whoever has completed the most instructions wins. Make sure you make plenty of instructions.

LET'S GET ACQUAINTED

The following list should be printed up and given to each person in the group. The idea is to fill in each blank on your sheet with someone who fits the description. The first person to get all his blanks filled, or the one who has the most at the end of the time limit is the winner. The sample list below is only a suggested list. Be creative and come up with some of your own. This is a good way for people to get to know each other a little better.

1. Find someone who uses Listerine ....
2. Find someone who has three bathrooms in his house ....
3. Find someone who has gotten more than two traffic tickets ....

4. Find someone who has red hair..
5. Find someone who gets hollered at for spending too much time in the bathroom
6. Find someone who has been inside the cockpit of an airplane...................
7. Find someone who play a guitar..
8. Find someone who likes "frog legs"...
9. Find someone who has been to Hawaii ....
10. Find someone who uses your brand of toothpaste.............................
11. Find someone who has used an "outhouse"......................................
12. Find a girl with false eyelashes on..
13. Find a guy who has gone water skiing and got up the first time...............
14. Find someone who knows what "charisma" means............................
15. Find someone who is on a diet...
16. Find a girl who uses a Lady Remington Shaver...................................
17. Find a guy who has a match with him..
18. Find someone who has his own private bath at home...........................
19. Find someone who didn't know your last name..................................
20. Find someone who has a funny sounding last name ....

MATCH MIXER

This is a great way to help people in a group get to know each other better. Give each person three slips of paper or 3 x 5 cards. Have everyone write one thing about themselves on each slip of paper. Suggested items could be:

1. The most embarrassing thing that ever happened to me.

2. My secret ambition

3. The person I admire most

4. If I had a million dollars I would. . . .

All the cards are collected and redistributed three to each person. No one should have one that they wrote themselves. On a signal, everyone then tries to match each card with a person in the room. They circulate around the room and ask each other questions to determine whose cards they have. The first to do so is the winner. All the players may be allowed to finish, and then share their findings with the rest of the group.

NAME GUESS

On slips of paper write different names of famous people and pin one to the back of each person, not letting them see who they are. Each person is to ask other group members questions which can be answered either yes or no to help him guess who he is. The first person to guess correctly wins and the last person is the loser.

NAME TAGS

Make large name tags for everyone in the group before a meeting. As people come in, hand each a name tag (with someone else's name). Each must then find the person whose name is on his tag. Throughout the meeting let other people write whatever they want on the name tags. This is a good way for people to meet other people on the group's first retreat, and also the people can see what impressions they already have made.

PEOPLE BINGO

Randomly select people's names to fill in each square on playing boxes below (one name to a square). The best way to do this is to give every person a playing card like the one illustrated below that is blank, then each person just looks around the room and puts someone's name in every square. Then, from a hat, randomly pull player's names and if a player has that person's name on his card he marks an "X" in the square. First person to fill in square horizontally, vertically, or diagonally, wins.

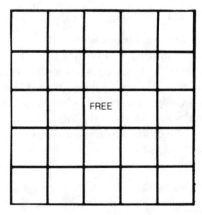

THE POINT GAME

Read a list similar to the one below and each person keeps track of his "points" as specified. Person with the most points wins.

1. 10 pts. if you are wearing red.
2. 10 pts. for every penny you have in your pocket.
3. 10 pts. if you have a white comb.
4. Your shoe size in points. ½ sizes get next highest points.
5. 15 pts. if your birthday is on a holiday.
6. 10 pts. if you have ridden on a train.
7. 10 pts. if you have a ball point pen.
   25 if it has red ink.
8. (Other items may be found in the "Sit Down Game") or dream some up!

SEVEN BEANS

This is a mixer that works best with big crowds. Everyone is given seven beans. The guests walk around the room asking each other questions. Every time they get the person they are talking to, to say either a yes or no, they win a bean from that person. The game continues for 10-15 minutes. The person with the most beans wins a prize.

THE SITUATION GAME

If you have your group sitting around in a circle, or in rows of chairs, this makes a fun game to liven things up. Have everyone whisper in the ear of the person to his right *who they are.* Have everyone be as creative as possible with this, and tell the person that they (the person getting told) are Batman, Brigitte Bardot, etc. Then have everyone tell the person to his left *where they are.* These should also be funny, such as "in the bathtub," "on top of a flagpole," etc. Then have everyone mix up and find new seats, and tell the person to the right of them *what they are wearing.* Then have everyone tell the person to his left *what they are doing.* After all this is done, have each person tell who they are, where they are, what they are wearing, and what they are doing. (They tell the things that the other people told them.) Such as, "My name is Phyllis Diller,

I'm wearing a purple bikini, and I'm in the bathroom, doing pushups." If you have a large crowd, appoint only a few to tell their story or ask for a few volunteers.

QUIET GAMES

QUIET GAMES

ART CHARADES

Teams play "charades" using the titles of pop songs (current hits) as titles to be guessed. Instead of "acting out" or using hand signals and pantomime, each player uses a piece of poster board and felt tip pens to describe the song title. No words may be used. Have each team select its "artist" and compete for fastest time.

ARTISTS' IMAGINATION

Divide into teams. Each team should have available a pencil and several pieces of paper. One member of each team is sent to the middle of the room where the leader quietly whispers one item that each must draw upon returning to his group. On signal, each representative returns to his team and without talking, or voicing any sound, begins drawing. Team members try to guess what the "artist" is drawing. The first team to shout out the correct item receives 50 points, the second 25. The "artist" may not write any words in his drawing, only pictures. Items to sketch could include:

Marcus Welby	the White House
a pizza	a coffeepot
a paper clip	a telephone
your youth director	a banana split
a mirror	the three bears
a tube of tooth paste	a gallon jug of root beer

BACK BREAK

Have a guy come to the front and lie down across the seats of three chairs, supported at his head, rear end, and his feet. He then must remove the middle chair (under his rear end) and lift it over his stomach and replace under his rear end from the other side while remaining supported only by his head and feet. If any part of his body touches the floor, he loses and gets a penalty. Have three guys do it for the fastest time.

BACKWARDS MOVIE

Obtain old silent action films in 16mm or 8mm from Blackhawk Films Eastin-Phelan Corp., Eastin Phelan Building, 1235 West 5th Street, Davenport, Iowa 52808. Hilarious effects can be had by running the film backwards.

BEAN BLITZ

This is a good way to get people involved with each other at the beginning of a meeting or social event. Each one is given an envelope containing 20 beans. The people then circulate around the room offering to someone else (one at a time) the opportunity to guess the number of beans in his closed hand. He approaches the person and says "Odd or Even." If the person guesses correctly, he gets the beans. If he guesses wrong, he must give up the same number of beans. A time limit is set, and whoever has the most beans at the end wins a prize. When your beans are all gone, you are out.

BOTTLE WALK

This really takes strength. All you need is a couple of soft drink bottles (regular size), a starting line, and markers or chalk. The contestants, with feet behind starting line and knees never touching the floor, grasp a bottle in each hand and "walk" on the bottles out as far as they can. Then they leave one bottle as far from the starting line as possible and "hop" back on the other bottle with both hands. The bottles must remain upright and the player must land on his feet, never having fallen. Carpeting is highly recommended. Height is a factor, but practice and technique count even more.

BUZZ

This is a good casual game to play indoors. Kids should be seated in a circle. Begin counting around the circle from 1 to 100. Whenever someone comes to a number containing a "7" or a *multiple* of seven, he says "Buzz" instead of that number. For example, it would go: 1,2,3,4,5,6, buzz, 8,9,10,11,12,13, buzz, 15,16, buzz, 18,19,20,buzz, 22, etc. You have to stay in rhythm, and if you make a mistake, or pause too long, you are out, or must go to the end of the line.

You can play "FIZZ" which is the same game, except that the number is "5" instead of "7." That makes the game easier for younger people. To really get the game complicated, play "*Fizz-Buzz*." Combine the two games. It would sound like this: 1,2,3,4,fizz,6,buzz,8,9,fizz,11,12,13,buzz,fizz,16,buzz,18,etc.

CONFUSION LANE

Have the kids sit in a semi-circle (like a horseshoe). The person on one end takes a pencil and hands it to the person sitting next to him and says, "Here is a pencil." That person says, "A what?", and the first person must tell him over again. The second person hands the pencil to the third and says, "Here is a pencil," and he says, "A what?", and the second person has to ask the first again, "A what?", and he repeats "A pencil," and the second person tells the third, "A pencil." This continues all the way around the semi-circle. The hard part, however, is that you start a *different* item in the same way from the other end of the line. When they meet in the middle, chaos breaks loose. Good luck.

DEAF AND MUTE MOTHER GOOSE

Divide the group into two teams, and have each team select from memory a Mother Goose rhyme, and act it out for the other team, without actually telling the other team which rhyme it is. The object is to get the other team to guess correctly the rhyme. If the game is to be a contest, divide the group into three teams. Each team is assigned a rhyme to act out. Another way to conduct this game is to have each acting team portray a rhyme selected by the opposing team.

DICTIONARY

Dictionary is a game that may be played by any number of people. All you need is a dictionary and a pencil, plus a 3 x 5 card for each participant.

One person looks up a word in the dictionary that he thinks no one will know what it means. He then asks the group if anyone knows it (to make sure no one does). He copies the correct definition on a 3 x 5 card, and then asks each participant to write as good a definition of the word as possible on his card. Each person signs his card.

The definitions are all collected and read to the group, along with the correct one. The object then is to guess the correct one. A point is given to each participant who guesses the right definition. A point is also given to each participant for every person who thinks his (wrong) definition is the correct one. The person choosing the original word is given 5 points if no one guesses the correct answer. (Noah Webster is the national grand champion at this game and as a result, several volumes of dictionaries have been named in his honor.)

DIME TRICK

Take a dime, wet it, and press it firmly against the forehead of a volunteer. Ask him to try to shake it off. The dime will stick with surprising strength, but he will be able to shake it off after a few tries. Try this with several volunteers, as a contest to see which player can shake it off in the fastest time. For fun, when you stick the dime on the last player's forehead, quickly take it off without his knowledge. It will feel like it is still there if you press firmly on his forehead. He will try to shake it off, but it just won't fall (because it's not there). You'll need to practice removing the dime ahead of time so that your volunteer doesn't suspect anything.

Some variations on this theme: The number of times it takes for you to shake the dime off is the number of years that will pass before you get married, the number of children you will have, the number of times you have been kissed, etc. Of course, the person with no dime on his forehead will have a very high number for his answer.

DO I KNOW THAT PERSON?

Divide the people into four groups. Have each group select one person and list 6-8 facts about him. Then have the recorder of the group read the facts to the other 3 groups. The object is to guess the person whom the facts describe as soon as possible.

DUCKIE WUCKIE

Everyone sits in a circle with one person standing in the middle. The person in the middle is blindfolded and has a rolled-up newspaper. He is spun around as everyone else changes seats. Everyone must be silent. The person blindfolded then finds a person's lap *only* by means of the end of the newspaper. Once a lap is found the newspaper is unfolded and placed on the lap. The blindfolded person sits on the newspaper and says "Duckie Wuckie." In a disguised voice the person being sat upon responds with "quack-quack." (Duckie wuckie and quack-quack may be repeated twice more.) After each "quack-quack," the blindfolded person may guess the identity of the voice. If guess is correct, the voice gets the blindfold, if incorrect the blindfold must find another lap and try again.

DUMB DOLORES

For a good way to break open a group who perhaps do not know each other very well, have all the people sit in somewhat of a circle. One person starts by giving his name, plus an adjective that begins with the first letter of his name. Some examples: Barfy Bob, Happy Harry, Awful Alan, etc. The next one repeats the guy's "name" and then gives his own same way. The game continues around the circle with each one having to remember everyone before him and then himself. The last guy must name everyone. The crazy thing is that these goofy names stick. For a long time people remember each other as "Weird Wayne" or "Beautiful Bill" or "Dumb Dolores." This should be restricted to groups of 30 or less.

GEIGER COUNTER

Everyone is seated in the room. The leader selects a "volunteer" to leave the room. While he is away, the group agrees on a hiding place for a random object, which the leader hides. The person returns and tries to find the object, not knowing what it is. The rest of the group, much like a geiger-counter "tick-tick-tick-ticks" slower as he moves away from the object and faster as he moves closer, until he finds it. Volunteers may compete for the fastest time.

HIDE THE LOOT

Make two simulated one-million-dollar bank notes on slips of paper, and hand one each to members of two teams. After one team leaves the room, have the other select a place to hide the "counterfeit" note. The other team, composed of "treasury agents," is then invited back in and allowed to ask questions. However, the questions may not be about specific areas of the room, and each question must be directed at a specific individual among the "counterfeiters" team, who must always answer the questions truthfully. Each treasury agent is allowed to ask as many questions as he wishes but whenever an agent decides to guess a specific location as the hiding place, he must announce that he is doing so — and, if he guesses wrong, he is eliminated from the game. After the hiding place is discovered, the first team leaves the room, and the other team hides its bank note, etc.

The object of the game is to eliminate all of the agents, or else keep them asking questions. If one team is able to eliminate all the agents, and the other cannot when the roles are switched, then the first team is the winner. Otherwise, the team which forces the other to ask the most number of questions before the hiding place was discovered is the winner.

The questions asked may be about the act of hiding the note, what the note is touching in its hiding place (wood, paper, leather, skin, etc.), and so on. For instance, an agent may ask, "Did the person who hid the note have to stand on tiptoes or on a chair to reach the hiding place?" Or, "Is the note lying directly under something?" The agents may not move around during the questioning, and may ask only those questions which can be answered by either "yes" or "no."

HIP CHARADES

This is a great game for casual get-togethers. It is played just like charades, except that team members spell out words with their *hips* instead of using pantomine or hand signals. Each contestant tries to get his team to guess the words he is spelling out by standing with his back to the team and moving his hips to form (or "write") the letters in the air. The team shouts out each letter as they recognize it and attempt to guess the correct title in the fastest time possible. The results are hilarious.

HOT POTATO

The "Ohio Art" Toy Company manufactures a toy game called the "Hot Potato" (or "Spudsie") that is a great game to use as a crowd-breaker. You wind it up and pass it around the group, and after 15 seconds or so, a bell rings inside the potato. Whoever is holding the potato at that time is the "loser" and receives a penalty of some kind, such as the "Hot Seat." When you pass it around, the following rules apply: (1) You may not throw it; (2) you must take it if someone hands it to you; (3) if you drop it, it is still yours until you pick it up and get it going again; and (4) you may hand it back to the person who gives it to you if you choose.

INDOOR GOLF

The room is arranged with as many folding tables as you have foursomes. Number the tables making the highest number the head table.

Partners remain together only for one game (hole). Total round consists of 9 or 18 games (holes).

One set of dice is needed for each table — the dice remain at that table.

A six must be rolled to start scoring — (partners count, too). Must be a six on one or both dice.

Only one roll or turn unless a score is made, then additional turns as long as you score.

Each person rolls separately but totals with his partner for that hole.

JINGLE JANGLE

Using old magazines, etc., cut out 2 different types of the same ad for all sorts of products, e.g. BOLD detergent. Take each person individually into a back room (or whatever is available) and pin an ad to his back. Have the person then match up with the other person who has on his back the same product. Next, they should get together and make up a 2-line or 4-line jingle advertising that product. Give each couple a chance to "sell" their product.

KILL THE UMPIRE

Two people are placed in the center of the room and are blindfolded. One is the Umpire, the other is the batter. The "umpire" gets a whistle, the "batter" gets a rolled-up newspaper. Every five seconds, the umpire must blow the whistle, and the batter tries to hit him with the newspaper. After several people have played (give each two players one or two minutes maximum), secretly remove the blindfold of one of the players.

KILLER

This is a highly successful game, great for small groups of less than forty people. Everyone sits in a circle (in chairs, or on the floor) and faces in. The leader has a deck of playing cards and he lets everyone in the room take one card without showing it to anyone. (There are only as many cards in the "deck" as there are people in the room.) One of the cards is a "Joker," and whoever draws it becomes the "killer." No one, of course, knows who the killer is except the killer himself. Play begins then, by everyone just looking around at each other and talking casually. The killer "kills" people by *winking* at them. When a person notices that he has been killed (winked at) he *waits ten seconds* and then says, "I'm dead." The object is to try and guess who the killer is before you get killed. Once you are winked at, you are dead and you can't reveal who did it to you. If you take a guess, and guess wrong, then you are dead, too. The killer tries to see how many people he can pick off before he gets caught. When he *is* caught, the cards are collected, shuffled and the game is repeated as many times as there is time.

MAD LIBS

This game is a great crowd breaker for any age group, and is available in book form from most book stores (not Christian) and stationery stores. "Mad Libs" are stories with certain key words left out, such as nouns, adjectives, and persons, and the audience supplies the words as they are asked for by the leader, without knowing anything about the story. The words the audience supplies should be as ridiculous as possible, and the leader writes them into the story as provided in the "Mad Libs" book. The results are always entertaining. The books are distributed by Pocket Books, Inc., 630 Fifth Ave., New York, and there are many editions of the game with titles such as *Mad Libs, Son of Mad Libs, Sooper Mad Libs*, etc.

MAP GAME

This is a good indoor game for small groups. Obtain several road maps (all identical) of your state (or any state, for that matter) and before the game draw, on just one of the maps, a

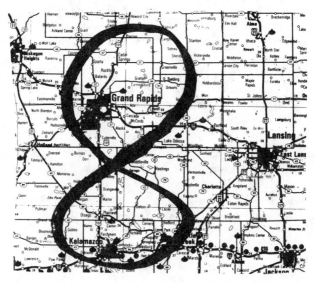

large number, letter, or symbol with a pencil, such as a number "8." Make a list of all the towns that your pencil line crosses or comes near. Have the kids divide up into small groups and give each group an unmarked map and the list of towns. On "Go" they must locate the towns on the map and figure out what the number or letter is that the towns form when connected with a line. No guessing allowed (a wrong guess disqualifies them) and the first group to come up with the correct answer wins.

MIND STOPPER

Form a circle. In the middle stands the person who is "it." He quickly points to someone in the circle and says, "This is my toe." At the same time he points to his chin with his other hand. The person pointed to must grab his toe and say, "this is my chin" before "it" counts to five. If the person pointed to goofs or doesn't make it by 5, he becomes "it."

MINDREADING GAMES

The following "mindreading" games are all basically alike. There are at least two people who are "clued in" and know how the game is played while the rest of the group is left in the dark. The idea is to try to guess the "code" that the mindreader and his clued-in partner are using to perform the trick involved. As soon as someone in the audience thinks they have the "code" figured out, then allow them to try it and see if they can do it. Keep going until most of the group has finally caught on or until you decide to reveal the code.

"BLACK MAGIC"

While mindreader is out of the room, the audience picks any object. The mindreader returns and the leader points to many different objects. The correct item is identified by the mindreader. *Code:* The chosen object is pointed to immediately *after* an object that is black has been pointed to.

"BOOK MAGIC"

Several books are placed in a row. One of them is chosen for the mindreader to guess when he returns to the room. The leader points to several books (apparently at random) and when he points to the correct book, the mindreader identifies it. *Code:* The chosen book follows any book pointed to that is on the end of the row.

"CAR"

While "mindreader" is out of the room, the crowd picks an object. The mindreader returns and is shown three objects. (One of the three is the correct one.) He correctly picks the chosen object. *Code:* The leader calls the mindreader into the room by making statements that begin with either the letters "C," "A," or "R." (Such as "Come in," "All right," or "Ready"). "C" indicates the first object shown, "A" the second, and "R" is the third object. So, when the mindreader is brought into the room, he knows automatically which object it will be.

"THE NINE MAGS"

Nine magazines are placed on the floor in 3 rows of 3. The mindreader leaves the room, and the crowd picks a magazine for the mindreader to identify when he returns. When he does return, the leader, using a pointer of some kind, touches various magazines in a random order, and when he touches the correct one, it is properly guessed. *Code:* The leader touches the very first magazine he points to in one of nine possible places:

1	2	3
4	5	6
7	8	9

Where the leader touches the *very first* magazine he points to shows the position of the selected magazine in the three rows of three. (For example, if the magazine in the # 9 position is "it," then whichever magazine the leader points to first will be touched in the lower corner corresponding to the #9 position.) After pointing to the first one, the leader then can point to as many magazines as he wants before pointing to the right one, as the mindreader already knows which one it is.

"RED, WHITE AND BLUE"

This is just like "Black Magic," only it is more confusing, and almost impossible to figure out if you don't know how it's done, and are watching it being performed. The first time the mind-reader tries to guess the chosen object, it immediately follows a red object. The next time, a white object, and the third time, a blue object. It just rotates, red-white-blue, etc.

MURDER

This is a great indoor game for casual get-togethers. Place a number of slips of paper in a hat. There should be the same number of slips of paper as there are players. One of these slips of paper has the word "detective" written on it, and another has the word "murderer" on it. The rest of them are blank. Every-one draws a slip of paper from the hat. Whoever drew the word "detective" announces himself, and it is his job to try to locate the murderer, who remains silent. From this point, there are two ways the game may be played:

1. The detective leaves the room, and the room is darkened. All the players mill about the room and the "murderer" silently slips up behind someone and very quietly whis-pers, "You're dead," in his ear. The victim counts to three, screams, and falls to the floor. The lights are turned on and the detective reenters the room. He then may question the players for one minute (or so) and tries to guess the identity of the murderer. If he is correct, the murderer becomes the detective, and a new murderer is selected. During the questioning, only the murderer may lie. All others must tell the truth, if they saw any-thing.

2. The detective remains in the room, and the murderer attempts to "murder" as many victims as possible (in the manner described above) before he is caught by the detective. The murderer gets points for every person he can kill before being discovered, and the detective gets points deducted for every incorrect guess or accusation. Everyone should get a chance to play both roles. This is best with at least twenty players.

OPEN OR CLOSED

This is a great game for small informal meetings in which kids sit around in a circle and pass around a book or a pair of scissors. When the object is passed, each person must announce whether he is passing it "open" or "closed." For example, he might say, "I received it (Open or Closed) and I am passing it (Open or Closed). The leader then tells the person whether he is right or wrong, and if he is wrong, he must sit on the floor or stand up (anything to look conspicuous). The idea is to learn what the "secret" is, namely this: If your *legs* are crossed, you must pass the object *closed*. If your legs are "open" (uncrossed), you must pass the object *open*. It sounds simple, but it really is tough to figure it out, and it makes for a real fun game.

QUICK-DRAW CONTEST

Place an easel with a drawing pad on it at the front of the room. Choose two couples and send them out of the room. The boy stands at the easel with a felt-tip pen, and the girl faces the audience and is given an object, such as a can opener, a light bulb, a screwdriver, etc. (The boy should not see what the object is.) The girl then tries to describe the object to the boy and he tries to draw it from her description, and guess what the object is. The girl may not use words that would give away what the object is, but must merely describe the shape of it, such as "Draw a straight line about three inches long, and then curve it slightly to the right . . ." With younger people, allow the girl to watch the boy as he draws, and give him instructions, correcting, etc. Time the first couple and then bring the second couple in and they do the same thing with the same object. Don't make the object *too* hard.

REVOLVING STORY

Begin at one side of the room or circle. The first person begins to make up a fairy tale of some kind. He continues for 10 seconds and at a signal the next person in line adds to the story for 10 seconds and so on down the line. The results are usually quite funny.

RHYTHM

Everyone in the room numbers off in a circle (1,2,3,4,etc.) with the #1 guy in the end chair. The "rhythm" is begun by the # 1 guy and everyone joins in by first slapping thighs, clapping hands, then snapping right hand fingers, then snapping left hand fingers in a continuous 1-2-3-4-1-2-3-4-1-2-3-4, etc. motion at a moderately slow speed. (It may speed up after everyone learns how to play.) The real action begins when the # 1 guy, on the first snap of the fingers, calls out his own number, and on the second snap of the fingers, calls somebody else's number. For example, it might sound something like this: (slap) (clap) "ONE, SIX!", and then the number six guy (as an example) might go: (slap) (clap) "SIX, TEN!", and then the number ten guy would do the same thing, calling out someone else's number on the second finger snap, and so on. If anyone misses, he goes to end and everyone who was after him before moves up one number. The object is to eventually arrive at the number one chair.

SKYDIVING LESSON

Three boys are chosen to learn how to skydive. One at a time, each boy is brought into the room and asked to stand on a sturdy 2 x 4 plank, which is lifted up by 2 strong boys. He uses the leaders' shoulders as a grace, so he won't fall. The board is lifted up about 3 feet, then the contestant is asked to jump into a small circle for five points. The board is lifted higher, and he jumps again for 10 points. The last times, for 20 points, he must jump blindfolded. The strong boys, however, only lift the board 2 or 3 inches, and the leader stoops down real low, giving the blindfolded contestant the feeling that he is high. He jumps, but usually falls flat on his face.

SPEECH SPASM

Have a volunteer come to the front and announce that he is going to be tested to see if he can earn a dollar bill. All he has to do is say two common, simple words: "Toy" and "Boat." He must say the two words ten times in five seconds *correctly* and he gets the dollar bill. Have him try the words separately to make sure he can pronounce them. (Have the audience applaud.) Then have him try it quickly as instructed. It is highly unlikely that he will be able to do so.

STINK

Put a dozen or so milk cartons on a table with various smelly things in each. Cover the top with cheesecloth or a nylon or something that will hide what's in the carton, but still allow the odor through. Number the cartons and let everyone take a guess, by putting his guess on paper. Announce the winner later on in the meeting, also announcing the smelly goodies.

Some samples:

Rotten egg	Fertilizer
Ammonia	Toothpaste
Coffee	Pizza
Mouthwash (Brand)	Paint thinner
Horseradish	Cigarette butt
Smelly sock or gym shorts	Fingernail polish

STORY LINE

The group is divided into two or more teams. Each team elects a "spokesperson" for its group. Each group then gets a card with a daffy sentence typed on it (create your own; the daffier the better). (Example: "Fourteen yellow elephants driving polka-dotted Volkswagens converged on the Halloween party.") The spokesperson from each group then comes forward with their card. The leader then explains that he/she will begin telling a story; at a certain point, he/she will stop and point to one of the "spokespersons" who will have to pick up the story line and keep it going. Every minute or so, a whistle will sound and that person must stop talking and the next "spokesperson" must pick up the story line. This continues for about 10 minutes. The object is to work the story line around so that you get the sentence you have been given into the story in such a way that the other groups cannot tell you have done so. At the end of the story, each group must decide whether the "spokesperson" for the other group was able to get their sentence into the story — and if so, what it was. Points may be awarded for getting sentence, guessing whether or not it got in and what the sentence was. (Example of beginning story line: "Dudley Do-Right and Priscilla Pure were rowing in the middle of the lake one fine summer day. Dudley had a passionate crush on Priscilla and longed to hold her fair soft hand. When no one was around, he pulled his oar in and reached out for Priscilla's smooth tender fingers. He was inches away when suddenly . . .")

SYMBOL RHYTHM

This is just like "Rhythm" except that instead of numbers, everyone has a "symbol" such as a cough, a whistle, scratching the head, etc. Instead of calling out numbers in rhythm, you give a signal, and everyone needs to be watching pretty closely. Everyone keeps the same signal throughout the game, but you change positions as you move up.

TOSS THE RAG

Tie a rag or sock into a tight knot. Everyone is seated in a circle with "it" in the middle. He tosses the rag to someone and shouts some category (like soft drinks, washing machines, presidents, birds, books of the Bible, etc.). He then counts to ten rapidly. If he reaches ten before the other person names an example of that category (Coke, Kenmore, Lincoln, Sapsucker, etc.), then that person takes his place in the center. The category named should be a "common noun," while the examples given are normally "proper nouns."

WHAT'S HIS CHOICE?

On large paper or cardboard compile two lists. The first list contains the names of 5 people or characters. The names may be fictional or real, living or historical. But they should be names most people are familiar with, e.g. Spiro Agnew, Mae West, Moses, Superman. The second list should include the following: What flavor ice cream? What kind of tree? What type of fabric? What make of car? What type of gem? What kind of building? What kind of bird? What kind of color?

Make copies of these two lists to match the number of teams you have determined. Each team is asked to spend 15 minutes in choosing one name from the list of characters and then attempting to match that character's personality or attributes to the second list of categories. At the end of 15 minutes each team reports back by reading down the list of categories what attributes they have agreed on, e.g., Tutti Futti Ice Cream, Weeping Willow, etc. The other teams must then guess which of the five characters this particular team is describing.

WINK

Chairs are arranged in a circle, facing inward. One boy stands behind each chair with his hands behind his back. Girls sit in the chairs, except for one chair left vacant. The boy behind that particular chair is "it." He must get a girl into that chair. He does this by winking at any one of the girls seated in the other chairs. She then tries to get out of the chair she is sitting in without the boy behind her tagging her on the back. If she is tagged, she must remain in her chair and "it" tries again, either by winking at another girl or the same one. If the girl winked at can get out of her chair without being tagged, she takes the chair in front of "it" and the boy with the vacant chair is now "it." The game proceeds in this manner. Anyone who can avoid becoming "it" is declared the winner. Halfway through the game, have the boys switch places with the girls.

WATER GAMES

WATER GAMES

CRAZY BOAT

This is a great game for a water carnival where you have a large pool or lake. Two boats are needed. Simply tie a rope between the two boats, place them in the center of the lake or racing area, and on the signal, the players in each boat try to reach their goal on opposite ends of the lake or pool. In other words, it's just a plain tug-o-war with boats. More than one boat may go on each end of the rope (end to end) if you have enough boats and room.

CRAZY CANOE

Two people get in a canoe facing each other. Each has a paddle. One paddles one direction, the other paddles the other way. The winner is the one who can paddle the canoe across his goal line about 20 feet away. The stunt is difficult as well as being hilarious to watch. The canoe tends to just go around in circles. This may be done in a large swimming pool. In a larger canoe, four or six people can play, with the two teams on each end of the canoe.

ICEBERG RELAY

This is a great idea for a swimming party. Players push or pull a twenty-five pound block of ice to the opposite end of a swimming pool and back. It's frigid. Use several blocks of ice and award prizes for the best time.

IN AND OUT RACE

This is a good game for a "water carnival," or anywhere there are water and boats. Several canoes or rowboats are required. Divide into several teams of five members each. Put each team in a separate rowboat and line the rowboats up evenly in a racing formation. Set up a finish line 50 yards down the course. At the signal, each boat team is to propel itself as far as possible using only their hands. (Oars are not allowed in the boat.) As the race progresses, the leader is to blow his whistle. Whenever the whistle is blown, all members of each team are to leap out of their boat into the water, climb back into the boat, wait until all members are in the boat, and then paddle on. Leaders are encouraged to blow their whistles often. After several times of "in and out," the boats swamp, and the race becomes a real test of nautical skill.

SURFBOARD RELAY

This is a great idea for a swimming party. Players line up and paddle to the opposite end of pool and back while lying backwards on surfboards. Paddling backwards is ridiculous and awkward so everyone gets a huge laugh as well as a good game.

SWEATSHIRT RELAY

The difficulty of this swimming pool relay is the changing of a wet sweatshirt. The object is to run through the water to a predetermined point and back, give the sweatshirt to the next contestant, and sit down. Obviously, if the sweatshirt is not changed correctly, the contestants may be there all day. The best way to get the sweatshirt from one person to the other is to have both contestants lean toward each other and hold hands with arms outstretched. The sweatshirt may then be pulled off one and onto the other easily by another teammate. (Contestants must have sweatshirt completely on before running into water.)

A SWIM PARTY IDEA

Call it what you like: an "Aquatic Carnival," a "Plunge Party," a "Pool Olympics," or whatever, but here are some more great water games.

1. *Candy Grab* — Toss wrapped candy in the pool (a lot) and kids jump into the pool and see who can retrieve the most.

2. *Wheelbarrow Race* — Divide into groups of two and one grabs the ankles of the other and pushes.

3. *Block Nudge* — Nudge a block (childrens' wooden alphabet type) with your nose to the other side of the pool.

4. *Frog Sub* — The opposite of leapfrog. Players pair off and alternate going through the other person's legs.

5. *Jelly Fish Float* — Float with face in the water with a 20-second time limit.

6. *Candle Race* — Light a candle and carry it across the pool (swimming or walking) and back. If the candle goes out, go back to the start and light it again.

7. *Dog Paddle Race* — Players dog paddle back and forth or make a four-man relay.

8. *Back Float* — Players float on their backs for time.

9. *Tread Water* — Players tread water (deep end of pool) for longest time.

10. *Somersault Race* — Players swim across the pool, but every time the whistle is blown, they must do a somersault in the water, then continue swimming.

WATER CARNIVAL

Next time you have a "pool party" or a swim meet at camp, try some of these games:

1. *Walk the Plank* — Tie a long narrow pole onto the diving board so that it extends out over the water. It may be fastened on with good rope. Mark it off at one foot intervals all the way out to the end of the pole. Kids then see who can walk out on it the farthest. The markings on the pole indicate how far each person gets.

2. *Ugly Dive Contest* — See who can do the craziest, most unusual dive. Have the non-participants judge.

3. *Cannonball* — See who can make the biggest splash off the board.

4. *Pearl Diving Contest* — Kids dive for money thrown into the pool. The team with the most money wins.

5. *Potato Race* — This is done in shallow water, but may be done in deep water if your players are good swimmers. Contestants carry a potato in a spoon to a goal and back, relay style. If the potato falls off, it must be picked up with the spoon. You may not touch the potato with your hands.

WATER DECATHLON

Divide into teams with 10 on each team. Ten places around the pool should be numbered (1-10) with the numbers clearly visible. Team members stand at each of the 9 stations and when their turn comes, they must wear a lifeguard hat (or some other hat) while participating in the event. The hat must be passed to the next person in line before he or she may perform the next event. The following is done by the team members. (Each does a different event, one after the other for time.)

1. Swim across the pool with an egg balanced on a spoon. (If the egg falls the swimmer must retrieve it and continue.)

2. Dive to the bottom of the pool and retrieve a brick.

3. Cross the pool hand-over-hand from a rope suspended over the water.

4. Swim across the pool with a tether ball tied to each ankle.

5. Two contestants have one ankle tied together and must swim in tandem across the pool.

6. Sit in an inner tube and hand-paddle backward across the pool. The tube must then be placed over a stake before the next team member starts.

7. Dive and swim underwater across the pool (side to side).

8. Dunk the leader in the pool. (Either have a regular dunking machine or some target the contestant must hit with a ball. The clothed leader may then be pushed backward off the diving board.)

9. Put on a large pair of pants, buckle the belt, and put on a long sleeve sweat shirt. The contestant must then swim across the pool with a beach ball for buoyancy and toss the

ball through designated goal posts. When the ball goes
through the goal posts, this stops the clock.

The team with the best time wins. Penalty seconds will be
given for holding the egg, not making the distance underwater,
etc.

INDEX

Outdoor
Scavenger Hunt - easy

comb
paperclip
dime
white string
2 belts tied together
unchewed stick
of gum
stick

ring
book
penny
sock
leaf
clover
rock

Timer/watch
earring
dark glasses
bracelet
rubber band
safety pin

Trivia

Have groups of 2 or 3 plus a
scorekeeper

Ask question of a group; if they
get the answer, they get a
point. If can't answer, some
other group get chance to
answer & get the point.
If a group answers out of
turn, take a point away.

20 Questions

Have categories, eg politics, sports,
entertainment, literature, TV

1 person from each team is
shown the answer; then that
person answers questions from
his team directed to him by a
team spokesperson

R. Reagan Ford. Marcos Wm. Perry Perry John McEnroe
Pete Rose Khadafy Sylvester Stallone

Wheel of Fortune

2 teams or more
On large piece of paper person makes
blanks for all the letters in a word or
phrase. Teams guess consonants 1 at a time to
see if they can guess word or phrase.
– – – – – – – –   Kentucky
– – – – – –   Derby